D0602898

WILLIAMS-SONOMA

Special Occasions

The Best of Williams-Sonoma Lifestyles Series

Special Occasions

GENERAL EDITOR
CHUCK WILLIAMS

RECIPE PHOTOGRAPHY
RICHARD ESKITE
JOYCE OUDKERK POOLE

Contents

Introduction

What makes an occasion special? First and foremost, it is the event being celebrated. But when the party is over, it is usually the celebration itself that is remembered. Making a nice meal and sharing it with family and friends always ensures a good time. But combining several dishes into an exciting menu and serving it with style can generate fond memories for years to come.

Whether you're celebrating a birthday, a graduation, or a new job, or you're just renewing old friendships, the chapters that follow will provide you with a wide range of recipes to fit the occasion, from soups, salads, and starters to main courses, side dishes, desserts, and beverages. In the next few pages, you'll find pointers on planning a menu, guidelines for preparing dishes in advance, suggestions for serving, and ideas for decorating—all designed to make hosting parties easier. Use these tips to take the stress out of entertaining and you'll enjoy every celebration you host as much as your guests will.

PLANNING AHEAD

The first key to entertaining with ease is to plan ahead. Few things are more important to the success of a party than a relaxed and convivial host. And nothing can fluster a host faster than frantic last-minute preparations or hurried cleanup before guests arrive.

Even before the number of guests is confirmed, you should begin planning your menu. When deciding which dishes to serve, keep in mind the nature of the occasion and the season. The incorporation of fresh seasonal ingredients in any menu will enhance the flavors of the dishes and make the event more memorable, whether you are serving grilled chicken and vegetables and a salad of red, ripe tomatoes at a midsummer birthday party or a roast rib of beef and creamy mashed potatoes at a midwinter holiday get-together. If you need a few ideas to get you started, take a look at the menu planning guide, pages 12–13.

Once you've decided on your menu, draw up a detailed list of what you'll need and shop for as many ingredients as possible in advance of the party. Next, read through the recipes carefully to see if you can prepare some of dishes, or even parts of dishes, ahead of time. Many of the recipes include handy make-ahead guidelines to help you with planning. Appetizers, soups, and desserts, in particular, can often be readied weeks in advance and frozen, and then thawed either the day before or the day of the party. For some recipes, you may be able to clean and chop some or all of the ingredients a day or two in advance, saving you valuable time when you're ready to cook.

MAKING IT FESTIVE

Initial impressions are important, so a warm welcome
and an attractively decorated house are good beginnings.
Even if the occasion is a casual one, you need to set
aside some time to dress up the party area and to
plan music that will complement the spirit of the
get-together. Also, think about what you'll be cooking
when the doorbell first rings, to make sure that the
aromas that greet your guests will spark a pleasant
rush of anticipation of the meal to come.

Of course, any decorations you use will depend on
the event you're celebrating. If it's Christmastime,
tiny twinkling lights, holly wreaths, and an old-
fashioned tree come immediately to mind. But other
get-togethers may require more thought. For example,
decorations for a birthday gathering should reflect the
person being feted, whether it is baseball memorabilia
for a serious sports fan or old movie posters for a film
enthusiast. You'll also need to pick out a good spot
for guests to put their gifts for the celebrant. If old
friends are gathering for a dinner party, you might
place photo albums of shared memories on the coffee
table, or assemble a slide show on your computer.
For a party commemorating a graduation or a job
promotion, consider visuals that recall the honoree's
achievements or that project his or her bright future.

SERVING WITH STYLE

You have two basic choices for serving, a sit-down meal or a self-service buffet. Although the idea of guests serving themselves may sound appropriate only if the gathering is informal, buffets can be laden with exquisitely prepared dishes that are anything but casual. A large buffet area is a wonderful canvas for all types of decorations. You might use candles to give the table and surroundings a cozy atmosphere. You can add a vase or two of flowers and maybe some ribbons for a festive note, always keeping in mind that staying with a palette of no more than two or three complementary colors is usually best.

Other decorative elements will depend on your overall theme and menu. Use your imagination for ideas that produce an attractive, unified look. For example, seashells and bits of driftwood might decorate the buffet table for a seafood barbecue, or citrus fruits and glossy green leaves for a wintertime party. Or, you can even dispense with the table altogether, especially if the party is outdoors. Try setting your platters and bowls on unexpected surfaces, such as hay bales for a country cookout, wine barrels for a vineyard lunch, or overturned baskets for a harvest celebration.

If you've decided on a sit-down meal, you'll want to create attractive place settings, whether fine china, silverware, and crystal for a formal gathering, or handsome everyday dishes, flatware, and festive glassware for a casual get-together. Party favors placed at each setting for guests to take home become lasting mementos of the occasion. Decorative matching place cards and elaborately folded napkins, or simply folded napkins with a single bloom tucked into the crease, are also nice additions.

A practical consideration when serving any meal, but especially a buffet-style meal, is how to keep finished dishes at their ideal temperature. Chafing dishes, electric burners, and even heat lamps are good ways to keep hot dishes hot. Chilled soups and some salads hold up best if their containers are nested in vessels of crushed ice, whether the foods are individually portioned or served in single large bowls.

***

This volume includes more than 150 delicious recipes for every part of a meal. Whether you're planning an elegant cocktail party with hors d'oeuvres passed on silver trays, a cozy weeknight buffet of soups and salads, a romantic dinner for two, or a Thanksgiving dinner for a dozen, there are recipes here to suit the get-together. Combined with tips on menu planning, decorating ideas, and serving guidelines, you have all you need to make every celebration a special occasion.

Menu Planning

The recipes in this book were developed to complement one another, resulting in scores of different menus for both small and large parties. The ten examples here represent only a handful of the many possible combinations. Feel free to use any or all of the recipes on any given occasion.

Evening Al Fresco

Layered Vegetable Terrine with
Mustard Vinaigrette

Chicken Paupiettes with
Lemon-Tarragon Sauce

Asparagus with Butter and Lemon

Oranges in Syrup

Romantic Evening
for Two

Camembert-Filled Artichoke Bottoms

Rosemary Lamb Chops

Haricots Verts with Toasted
Almond Butter

Pears Poached in Red Wine

Weekend with Friends

Gougères

Tomato Soup with Minted Goat Cheese

Winter White Lasagna

Caramelized Pear, Lemon,
and Currant Tart

Traditional Thanksgiving Dinner

Belgian Endive, Celery Root, and Pear Salad

Roasted Butternut Squash Soup

Roast Turkey with Barley Stuffing

Cranberry Sauce

Favorite Pumpkin Pie

Late-Night Supper

Potato Pancakes with Smoked Salmon

Watercress, Pear, and Goat Cheese Salad

Lobster with Cognac Butter

Cranberry-Raspberry Granita

Black Tie Christmas

Herbed Mushroom and Chestnut Crepes

Seafood Bisque

Roast Duck with Cranberry Glaze

Warm Gingerbread

Springtime Celebration

Escarole Soufflé

Baked Ham with Orange-Mustard-Pepper Glaze

Ginger-Glazed Vegetables

Coconut Meringue Nests

New Year's Eve Cocktails

Oysters with Fresh Horseradish

Gorgonzola, Apple, and Pecan Filo Rolls

Deviled Crab Cakes

Crostini with Chicken Livers

Holiday Cosmopolitans

Apricot Champagne Cocktails

Seaside Lunch

Deviled Crab Cakes

Arugula and Orange Salad

Gazpacho

Petrale Napoleans with Ratatouille Confit

Sunday Brunch

Gruyère Herb Puffs

Confetti Crabmeat Soufflé Roll

Fingerling Potato Salad with Shrimp and Baby Dill

Champagne with Raspberries

Starters

Root Vegetables in Filo Packets

This delicate preparation features the best of winter's root vegetables and makes an elegant first course for any occasion. For added flair, garnish each golden packet with fresh sprigs of thyme or winter savory.

Cut off the stems, feathery tops, and any bruised outer stalks from the fennel bulb. Cut the fennel bulb, carrots, parsnips, potatoes, turnips, and onions into $1/2$-inch (12-mm) cubes. Place in a large bowl. Add the leeks, olive oil, and the herb sprigs. Sprinkle with the salt and pepper, toss gently, and let stand for 1 hour.

Preheat an oven to 350°F (180°C). Using a slotted spoon, transfer the vegetables to a baking sheet and spread them out in a single layer. Reserve the olive oil left behind in the bowl for basting. Roast, turning occasionally and basting with the reserved oil, until soft and tender, about 1 hour. Remove from the oven and let cool completely. Discard the herb sprigs.

Line 2 baking sheets with parchment (baking) paper. Cut the filo sheets in half crosswise. Working with a half sheet at a time, place on a work surface; keep the other sheets covered with a damp kitchen towel. Put $1/3$ –$1/2$ cup (2–3 oz/60–90 g) roasted root vegetables in the center of the sheet and dot with 1 tablespoon of the goat cheese. Fold in each side over the filling, then fold in the open ends, forming a square. Brush the square with melted butter and place, folded side down, in the center of another sheet. Wrap again in the same way, then brush the square with melted butter. Place, folded side down, on yet another half sheet, wrap, and brush again with the melted butter. Repeat a fourth time and again brush with melted butter. Place on the lined baking sheet. Repeat to make a total of 12 packets.

Bake until the filo is golden brown and crisp, about 25 minutes. Transfer the packets to a platter and serve at once.

Makes 12 packets; serves 6–8

1 large fennel bulb, about 1 lb (500 g)

6 carrots, about 1 lb (500 g) total weight, peeled

3 parsnips, about $1^1/2$ lb (750 g) total weight, peeled

4 potatoes, about $3/4$ lb (375 g) total weight, unpeeled

4 turnips, about 1 lb (500 g) total weight, peeled

1 yellow onion, about $1/2$ lb (250 g)

3 leeks, about 2 lb (1 kg) total weight, halved lengthwise, and thinly sliced

$1/2$ cup (4 fl oz/125 ml) extra-virgin olive oil

8 fresh thyme sprigs

8 fresh winter savory sprigs

1 teaspoon salt

2 teaspoons ground pepper

24 sheets filo dough, thawed if frozen

2 oz (60 g) fresh goat cheese

$1/4$ cup (2 oz/60 g) unsalted butter, melted

Cornmeal-Crusted Oysters with Sour Cream and Caviar

Oysters are a delicacy traditionally enjoyed with a glass of sparkling wine—what better way to kick off a holiday feast? Fried oysters are a great alternative to raw for people who love oysters but prefer them cooked.

24 oysters, shucked, with 4–6 shells reserved

½ cup (2½ oz/75 g) yellow cornmeal

½ cup (2½ oz/75 g) all-purpose (plain) flour

¾ teaspoon salt

½ teaspoon cayenne pepper

¼ teaspoon ground black pepper

2 eggs

Vegetable oil for frying

1 cup (8 fl oz/250 ml) sour cream

2 oz (60 g) black caviar, or to taste

Fresh flat-leaf (Italian) parsley sprigs

Preheat an oven to 200°F (95°C).

Drain the oysters and blot on a double thickness of paper towels to remove excess moisture. On a sheet of waxed paper, combine the cornmeal, flour, salt, cayenne pepper, and black pepper. In a shallow bowl, whisk the eggs until blended.

One at a time, roll the oysters in the cornmeal mixture, shaking off the excess. Dip them into the eggs and then roll them again in the cornmeal mixture to coat lightly. Place on a tray or platter, then refrigerate until ready to fry. (This can be done up to 1 hour before frying.)

Pour vegetable oil to a depth of 1 inch (2.5 cm) in a large frying pan and place over medium heat. To test if the oil is hot enough, drop a tiny crust of bread into it; it should sizzle upon contact. Add the oysters, 6–8 at a time, and fry, turning once, until golden, about 4 minutes. Using tongs or a slotted spoon, transfer to paper towels to drain. Keep warm until all are cooked. Repeat with the remaining oysters.

To serve, spoon the sour cream into the reserved oyster shells, dividing it evenly, and top each with a small spoonful of caviar. Place a shell in the center of each individual plate. Surround with the hot oysters. Garnish with a parsley sprig.

Serves 4–6

Oysters with Fresh Horseradish

Fresh horseradish has a fiery potency that marries well with raw oysters. Look for oysters and horseradish in well-stocked markets during the cooler months. To hold oysters steady on serving trays, nestle them into beds of crushed ice or rock salt.

Grip an oyster, flat side up, with a folded kitchen towel. Push in the tip of an oyster knife to one side of the hinge located on the narrow end and pry upward to open the shell. Run the knife blade all along the inside of the top shell to sever the muscle that joins the shells. Discard the top of the shell. Then carefully run the knife underneath the oyster to detach it from the bottom shell. Try not to lose any of the flavorful juices in the shell. Arrange the oysters in their bottom shells on trays or individual plates. Refrigerate until serving.

Using a knife or vegetable pepper, peel away the dark, rough skin from the horseradish. On the small holes of a handheld grater, grate enough of the root to measure about 1 cup (5 oz/155 g). Transfer the horseradish to a small serving bowl. To make a sauce, add the cream and stir well.

Serve the oysters on the half shell with the sauce and the lemon wedges alongside. Encourage guests to spoon about 1 teaspoon sauce onto each oyster before eating.

Serves 4

4 dozen oysters, well scrubbed

1 horseradish root, about 1/2 lb (250 g)

1/4 cup (2 fl oz/60 ml) heavy (double) cream (optional)

1 lemon, cut into wedges (optional)

Yukon Gold Potato Pancakes with Chives, Smoked Salmon, and Sour Cream

Crisp potato pancakes, or *latkes*, are classics of the Hanukkah table. Veteran latke makers say the secret to perfect crisp potato pancakes is to squeeze as much moisture as possible from the grated potato, and to fry the pancakes in vegetable shortening.

1³/₄ lb (875 g) Yukon gold or other yellow-fleshed potatoes, peeled

1 small yellow onion, grated

1 egg, lightly beaten

2 tablespoons matzo meal

1 teaspoon salt

Ground pepper to taste

2 tablespoons snipped fresh chives, plus extra for garnish (optional)

¹/₂ cup (4 oz/125 g) solid vegetable shortening, or as needed

2 oz (60 g) sliced smoked salmon, cut into 1-inch (2.5-cm) squares

¹/₄ cup (2 fl oz/60 ml) sour cream

Salmon caviar (optional)

Using the medium-fine holes of a handheld grater, grate the potatoes into a large bowl. Transfer to a sieve and, using the back of a spoon, press out the excess moisture. Then squeeze the potatoes with your hand to extract more moisture.

Place the grated potatoes in a bowl and add the onion, egg, matzo meal, salt, and pepper. Stir to blend. Fold in the 2 tablespoons chives.

In a heavy frying pan over medium-high heat, melt the ¹/₂ cup (4 oz/125 g) shortening until the surface ripples. Working in batches and being careful not to crowd the pan, measure out 1 level tablespoon batter for each pancake and drop it into the hot oil. Fry until crisp and golden on the first side, about 4 minutes. Turn and fry on the second side until golden, about 4 minutes longer. Transfer to paper towels to drain. Keep warm until all the batter has been used. Add more shortening to the pan if needed.

When all the pancakes have been cooked, arrange on a warmed platter. Top each with a square of smoked salmon, and then top the salmon with ¹/₂ teaspoon sour cream. If desired, sprinkle each with a few pieces of the remaining snipped chives or a small spoonful of caviar. Serve warm.

Makes about 24 bite-sized pancakes; serves 6–8

Gorgonzola, Apple, and Toasted Pecan Filo Rolls

The rich flavor of toasted nuts enhances this special holiday treat. You can vary the filling according to your own tastes. Try walnuts in place of the pecans, Roquefort in place of the Gorgonzola, and pears in place of the apples.

Preheat an oven to 350°F (180°C). Lightly butter a large baking sheet. In a small, dry frying pan over low heat, toast the pecans, stirring continuously, until light golden brown and fragrant, about 8 minutes. Transfer to a plate and set aside.

In a bowl, combine the apple, cheese, and flour and toss to mix well. Place a damp kitchen towel over the stack of filo to prevent the sheets from drying out.

Lay a large sheet of waxed paper on a work surface. Place a filo sheet on top. Using a wide pastry brush, coat with a thin film of the melted butter. Top with a second filo sheet and then a third one, buttering each sheet.

Sprinkle the buttered filo evenly with half of the pecans, then scatter half of the apple-cheese mixture over the nuts, distributing it evenly. Add a grinding of pepper. Top with 3 more filo sheets, brushing each one with the butter.

Starting from a long side, carefully roll up the filo layers as tightly as possible. Slide the roll onto the prepared baking sheet. Repeat with the remaining ingredients to make a second roll. Using a sharp, thin-bladed knife, cut about three-fourths of the way through the rolls at 1-inch (2.5-cm) intervals. This will make them easier to cut and serve after they are baked.

Bake until golden, about 25 minutes. Remove from the oven and let cool completely on the baking sheet. Carefully slide the rolls onto a cutting board and finish cutting into pieces.

Arrange the pieces, cut sides up, on a platter. Serve at once.

Makes 24 pieces; serves 8–12

1 cup (4 oz/125 g) pecans, finely chopped

1 cup (4 oz/125 g) peeled, cored, and finely chopped Golden Delicious or other firm cooking apple

1/4 lb (125 g) Gorgonzola cheese, crumbled

2 tablespoons all-purpose (plain) flour

12 sheets filo dough, thawed in the refrigerator if frozen

1/2 cup (4 oz/125 g) unsalted butter, melted and cooled

Freshly ground pepper to taste

Crisp Corn Fritters

These crisp, thyme-laced fritters work equally well as a simple first course, or in a pretty basket as a tasty alternative to rolls. They are also delicious served in the morning. You might try them as part of a holiday breakfast buffet.

8 ears of corn

1 or 2 jalapeño chiles, seeded and minced

1–2 tablespoons chopped fresh thyme or 1 teaspoon dried thyme

1/2 teaspoon ground black pepper

1/2 teaspoon ground white pepper

1/4 teaspoon red pepper flakes

4 eggs

1 1/2 cups (12 fl oz/375 ml) milk

1 1/2 cups (7 1/2 oz/235 g) all-purpose (plain) flour

1 tablespoon granulated sugar

1 teaspoon baking powder

1/4 teaspoon salt

About 1/4 cup (2 fl oz/60 ml) corn oil

2 tablespoons confectioners' (icing) sugar, for dusting

Working with 1 ear of corn at a time, hold the ear by its pointed end, steadying the stalk end in the bottom of a shallow bowl. Using a sharp knife, cut down along the ear to strip off the kernels, turning the ear with each cut. Then run the dull side of the knife blade along the ear, scraping out all of the pulp and milk. Stir in the chiles, thyme, black and white peppers, and red pepper flakes, mixing well.

In another bowl, whisk the eggs until frothy. Whisk in the milk, flour, granulated sugar, baking powder, and salt until well blended. Stir the egg mixture into the corn mixture.

Heat a large, heavy frying pan or griddle over high heat until a few drops of water flicked onto the surface skitter across it. Add about 1 teaspoon of the oil to the pan and, working in batches, drop the batter by tablespoonfuls onto the hot surface. Fry, turning once, until golden brown, about 1 minute on each side. Transfer to paper towels to drain and keep warm. Repeat until all the batter is cooked, adding oil to the pan as needed.

Dust the fritters with the confectioners' sugar, arrange in a napkin-lined platter or basket, and serve at once.

Makes 3–4 dozen 3-inch (7.5-cm) fritters

Creamy Butternut Squash Rounds

The butternut is one of the most dense-fleshed, flavorful squashes. Its nutty flavor adapts to a variety of preparations. These chutney-laden rounds make an elegant first course.

Preheat an oven to 350°F (180°C). Using a sharp knife, puncture the squash in 4 or 5 places. Put the squash on a baking sheet. Bake until very tender, 2–2 1/2 hours.

Meanwhile, make the chutney: In a heavy, nonaluminum saucepan, combine the peaches, plums, grapes, onions, brown sugar, currants or raisins, ginger, garlic, cayenne pepper, and vinegar. Place the cinnamon sticks, peppercorns, and cloves on a square of cheesecloth (muslin) and tie the corners securely with kitchen string. Add to the saucepan. Bring to a boil over high heat, stirring often. Reduce the heat to low and simmer, uncovered, stirring occasionally, until the mixture develops a loose, jamlike consistency, 50–60 minutes. Stir often during the last 10–15 minutes to prevent burning. Remove from the heat and let cool. Discard the cheesecloth bag. You will need about 1/2 cup (4 oz/155 g) of the chutney; reserve the remainder for another use. It will keep tightly covered in the refrigerator for up to 2 months.

Remove the squash from the oven and let cool for about 10 minutes. Cut in half lengthwise and discard the seeds and any fibers. Then scoop out the hot flesh and put it in a warmed bowl. Add the 2 tablespoons butter and the salt. Stir until the butter has melted and the squash is creamy.

Butter the inside of a round biscuit cutter 4 inches (10 cm) in diameter and 1 1/2 inches (4 cm) deep. Place on a warmed individual plate. Fill it with the hot squash, then lift the cutter straight up, leaving a tidy round of squash. Make 3 more molds on 3 more plates. Place 2 tablespoons chutney on top of each round and serve.

Serves 4

1 butternut squash, about 3 lb (1.5 kg)

FOR THE CHUTNEY

1 1/2 lb (750 g) peaches, peeled, pitted, and coarsely chopped

1/2 lb (250 g) plums, halved, pitted, and coarsely chopped

1/2 lb (250 g) seedless grapes, stems removed

2 yellow onions, chopped

1 3/4 cups (13 oz/410 g) firmly packed brown sugar

1 cup (6 oz/185 g) raisins or currants

1/4 cup (1 1/4 oz/37g) peeled and minced fresh ginger

4 cloves garlic, minced

1 teaspoon cayenne pepper

1 1/2 cups (12 fl oz/375 ml) apple cider vinegar

3 cinnamon sticks

1 tablespoon *each* peppercorns and whole cloves

2 tablespoons unsalted butter

1/4 teaspoon salt

Herbed Mushroom and Chestnut Crepes

Serve these crepes as a prelude to an elegant fall dinner. Look for fresh chestnuts in autumn and throughout the holiday season. If they cannot be found, substitute ¾ pound (375 g) canned chestnuts. Garnish with snipped chives or minced thyme.

To make the crepe batter, combine the flour, broth, eggs, and 2 tablespoons melted butter in a blender or food processor. Process until smooth. Transfer to a bowl. Stir in the chives and thyme. Cover and chill for at least 1 hour or for up to 12 hours.

Meanwhile, to roast the chestnuts, preheat an oven to 450°F (230°C). Using a sharp knife, score an X in the shell on the flat side of each chestnut, then place in a baking pan large to hold them in a single layer. Add water to the pan to form a very shallow pool in the bottom. Bake until the shells begin to open up at the Xs, 10–20 minutes. Remove from the oven and, while the nuts are still warm, peel off the brittle shells and the furry skin directly beneath them. Coarsely chop the nuts.

Place an 8-inch (20-cm) nonstick frying pan over medium heat. When the pan is hot, brush with melted butter. Stir the batter and pour ¼ cup (2 fl oz/60 ml) of it into the pan. Tilt the pan to create a thin, even layer of batter. Quickly loosen the edges with a spatula and cook until the top is set and looks dry, about 1 minute. Turn and cook just to brown lightly on the second side, 15–30 seconds longer. Transfer to a plate and repeat with the remaining batter. Stack the crepes between sheets of waxed paper as they are cooked. You should have 16 crepes in all.

In a sauté pan over medium heat, warm the olive oil. Add the green onions and sauté until softened, 2–3 minutes. Add the chestnuts and mushrooms and cook, stirring occasionally, until most of the mushroom liquid has evaporated, 8–10 minutes. Add the cooked rice, parsley, and marjoram and heat through. Season with salt and pepper.

Makes 16 filled crepes; serves 6

FOR THE CREPES

1 cup (5 oz/155 g) all-purpose (plain) flour

1 cup (8 fl oz/250 ml) vegetable broth

3 eggs

2 tablespoons unsalted butter, melted, plus extra for cooking

3 tablespoons finely snipped fresh chives

2 teaspoons minced fresh thyme

FOR THE FILLING

1 lb (500 g) chestnuts

3 tablespoons olive oil

4 green (spring) onions, sliced

1 lb (500 g) fresh mushrooms, brushed clean, stemmed, and thinly sliced

1 cup (7 oz/220 g) cooked brown rice

1 tablespoon minced fresh flat-leaf (Italian) parsley

1 teaspoon minced fresh marjoram

Salt and ground pepper to taste

Mushroom Crostini

Use any combination of fresh mushrooms as long as the total weight is 1 pound (500 g). Both the crostini and mushroom spread can be made ahead, which makes this a perfect recipe for the busy holiday cook. Garnish with fresh parsley, if you like.

FOR THE CROSTINI

1/2 cup (4 fl oz/125 ml) olive oil

24 slices coarse country bread

1 clove garlic, halved

FOR THE MUSHROOM SPREAD

1/2 lb (250 g) fresh white button mushrooms

1/4 lb (125 g) fresh cremini mushrooms

1/4 lb (125 g) fresh shiitake mushrooms

5 tablespoons (3 fl oz/80 ml) extra-virgin olive oil

2 cloves garlic, finely chopped

2 tablespoons finely chopped fresh flat-leaf (Italian) parsley

2 teaspoons fresh thyme leaves

1/2 teaspoon minced fresh rosemary

1 teaspoon coarse salt, plus salt to taste

Ground pepper to taste

1/4 cup (11/4 oz/37 g) drained, oil-packed sun-dried tomatoes, finely chopped

Preheat an oven to 350°F (180°C). To make the crostini, lightly brush olive oil on both sides of each bread slice. Arrange the bread in a single layer on a baking sheet.

Bake until the crostini are golden on the edges, about 25 minutes. Remove from the oven and let cool slightly. Using the cut side of the garlic, lightly rub one side over each slice of bread. Set aside. The crostini can be made up to 1 week ahead and stored in an airtight container.

To make the mushroom spread, brush the mushrooms clean, discard any stems, and chop. Heat 2 tablespoons of the olive oil in a large frying pan over medium-high heat. Add all the mushrooms and cook, stirring often, until lightly browned, about 10 minutes. Add the garlic, chopped parsley, thyme, rosemary, 1 teaspoon salt, and pepper. Cook, stirring, for 2 minutes longer.

Transfer the mushroom mixture to a food processor. Process until very finely chopped. With the processor running, add the remaining 3 tablespoons olive oil in a thin, steady stream, processing until the mixture is smooth and spreadable. Transfer to a bowl and stir in the chopped sun-dried tomatoes. Season with salt and pepper. The mushroom spread can be made up to 1 day ahead and stored, covered, in the refrigerator. Bring to room temperature before serving.

Spread each piece of bread with about 1 tablespoon of the mushroom mixture. Arrange on a platter and, if desired, garnish each with a parsley leaf and/or a sliver of sun-dried tomato.

Makes 24 crostini; serves 12

Potato Latkes

Although these potato pancakes are traditionally served during Hanukkah, they are a crowd pleaser any time of the year. Applesauce and sour cream are favorite toppings.

1 egg

2 medium baking potatoes, peeled and quartered

1 very small yellow onion, cut into chunks

3 tablespoons all-purpose flour

1/4 teaspoon salt

Big pinch of pepper

Dash ground nutmeg

Vegetable oil for cooking

Applesauce or sour cream for serving (optional)

In a blender, combine the egg, potatoes, onion, flour, salt, pepper and nutmeg. Blend just until the potatoes and onions are coarsely chopped and the ingredients are mixed, stopping to scrape down the side of the blender with a spatula if needed.

Put a few paper towels on the large plate; set the plate on your kitchen counter near your stove. Pour enough oil into the large, heavy frying pan to form a thin layer. Set the pan on your stove and turn the heat on to medium-high. Heat the oil until it is hot. To make each pancake, gently drop about $1/4$ cup of the potato mixture into the frying pan. Make only a few pancakes at a time and do not crowd the pan. With the metal spatula, lightly flatten the top of each pancake. Fry until golden brown on the underside, 2 to 3 minutes. With the spatula, turn each pancake over and fry until brown on the second side, 2 to 3 minutes longer. (The first batch might be hard to turn over, but the second batch will be easier.) With the spatula, carefully transfer the pancakes to the paper towels. Keep warm. Continue making the pancakes until all the batter has been used.

Serve the hot pancakes with applesauce or sour cream, if you like.

Serves 4

Gougères

Made from *pâte à choux*, the same dough that is used for cream puffs, these savory cheese pastries are a specialty of France's Burgundy region. They are best served warm from the oven.

Preheat an oven to 375°F (190°C). Line two baking sheets with parchment (baking) paper.

In a heavy saucepan over high heat, combine the 2 cups (16 fl oz/500 ml) milk, the butter, and salt. Bring to a boil and then add the flour all at once. Reduce the heat to low and stir until the mixture forms a ball and pulls cleanly away from the sides of the pan, about 5 minutes. Remove from the heat. Using an electric mixer set on medium speed, beat in the eggs, one at a time, until the paste is very shiny, about 5 minutes. Fold in three-fourths of the cheese after the last egg has been added.

Using a large tablespoon with an oval bowl, scoop out 2–3-inch (5–7.5-cm) rounds of dough onto the baking sheets, spacing them about 2 inches (5 cm) apart. Brush the rounds with the 2 tablespoons milk and sprinkle with the remaining cheese.

Bake until well puffed and browned, 30–35 minutes. Remove from the oven and let cool for 5 minutes before serving.

Serves 6–8

2 cups (16 fl oz/500 ml) plus 2 tablespoons milk

1/2 cup (4 oz/125 g) unsalted butter

2 teaspoons salt

2 cups (10 oz/315 g) all-purpose (plain) flour

8 eggs

1/2 lb (250 g) Emmentaler, Gruyère, or other Swiss-type cheese, finely diced

Gruyère Herb Puffs

These are easy to make ahead. Bake as directed, let cool, then freeze in a single layer.
Transfer to a lock-top bag and freeze for up to 4 weeks; thaw at room temperature,
then place on a baking sheet in a 350°F (180°C) oven for 10 minutes.

1/4 cup (2 oz/60 g) unsalted butter

1/2 cup (4 fl oz/125 ml) water

2/3 cup (3 1/2 oz/105 g) all-purpose (plain) flour

1/2 teaspoon salt

3 eggs, at room temperature

1 cup (4 oz/125 g) shredded Gruyère cheese

1 tablespoon fresh thyme leaves

1 teaspoon minced fresh rosemary leaves

1 teaspoon hot-pepper sauce, such as Tabasco

Preheat an oven to 400°F (200°C). Butter a large baking sheet.

In a saucepan over medium heat, combine the butter and water. Heat until the butter melts and the water boils, about 3 minutes. Add the flour and salt and stir vigorously with a wooden spoon until the mixture leaves the sides of the pan and forms a ball. Remove from the heat and let cool for 3 minutes.

Using a wooden spoon or a handheld electric mixer on medium speed, beat in the eggs, one at a time, beating well after each addition. The batter should have a dull sheen. Stir in the cheese, thyme, rosemary, and hot-pepper sauce until well mixed.

Drop the batter by rounded tablespoonfuls onto the prepared baking sheet, allowing about 2 inches (5 cm) between the mounds. Alternatively, spoon the batter into a pastry (piping) bag fitted with a large rosette tip and pipe mounds of batter onto the baking sheet.

Bake for 15 minutes. Reduce the oven temperature to 350°F (180°C) and continue to bake until puffed and golden, about 15 minutes longer. Remove from the oven and let cool on the baking sheet set on a rack. Arrange in a basket or on a tray. Serve warm or at room temperature.

Makes 24 puffs; serves 6–8

Crostini with Sweet-and-Sour Chicken Livers

In Italy, crostini are used as a base for everything from wilted greens and white beans to Gorgonzola, prosciutto, salt cod, and *fegatini agrodolce*, sweet-and-sour chicken livers. Offer this Tuscan specialty with a glass of full-bodied Chianti.

In a frying pan over medium heat, warm 1 tablespoon of the olive oil. Add the pancetta and sauté until golden and the fat is rendered, about 5 minutes. Add the onion and chopped sage and cook, stirring occasionally, until the onion is soft, about 10 minutes. Add the Marsala or white wine and simmer until it evaporates, 2–3 minutes. Transfer the mixture to a cutting board and mince. Place in a bowl and set aside.

In the same pan over low heat, warm the remaining 2 tablespoons olive oil. Place the livers in the pan in a single layer and cook until they start to turn golden, 2–3 minutes. Turn the livers over and continue to cook until firm to the touch yet still pink on the inside, 2–3 minutes longer. Season with salt and pepper. Transfer to a cutting board and let cool for 15 minutes.

Preheat a broiler (griller).

When the livers are cool, chop coarsely and add to the bowl with the pancetta mixture. Add the garlic, capers, and balsamic vinegar. Season with salt and pepper.

Arrange the bread slices on a baking sheet, slip under the broiler (griller), and toast, turning once, until golden, 30–60 seconds on each side.

Spread the liver mixture on the warm bread slices. Arrange on a platter, garnish with sage leaves, if using, and serve at once.

Serves 6

3 tablespoons extra-virgin olive oil

2 oz (60 g) pancetta, finely chopped

1/4 cup (1 1/2 oz/45 g) finely chopped yellow onion

1 teaspoon chopped fresh sage, plus small whole leaves for garnish (optional)

2 tablespoons dry Marsala or dry white wine

1/2 lb (250 g) chicken livers, trimmed of fat and sinew

Salt and ground pepper to taste

1 clove garlic, minced

1 tablespoon capers, chopped

1 tablespoon balsamic vinegar

12 slices coarse country bread, each about 3 inches (7.5 cm) in diameter and 1/4 inch (6 mm) thick

Deviled Crab Cakes

A tangy red pepper aoili makes a nice dip for these crispy cakes. For a simple aioli, try mixing roasted red pepper puree, garlic puree, and lemon juice into plain mayonnaise. Season to taste with salt, transfer to a small bowl, and serve alongside.

2 tablespoons unsalted butter

1 yellow onion, finely minced

2 celery stalks, chopped

2 teaspoons dry mustard

1/4–1/2 teaspoon cayenne pepper

1 lb (500 g) lump crabmeat, picked over for shell fragments

1/4 cup (2 fl oz/60 ml) mayonnaise

1 egg, lightly beaten

6 tablespoons (3/4 oz/20 g) fresh bread crumbs

3 tablespoons chopped fresh flat-leaf (Italian) parsley

1 teaspoon grated lemon zest

Salt and ground black pepper to taste

1 cup (4 oz/125 g) fine dried bread crumbs

2–4 tablespoons olive oil

In a medium sauté pan over medium heat, melt the butter. Add the onion and celery and sauté until softened, about 5 minutes. Add the mustard and cayenne, stir well, and cook, stirring occasionally, about 2 minutes longer to blend in the spices. Transfer to a bowl and let cool to room temperature or refrigerate.

When cool, stir in the crabmeat, mayonnaise, egg, fresh bread crumbs, parsley, and lemon zest. Season with salt and pepper.

Spread the dried bread crumbs on a plate. Line a baking sheet with parchment (baking) or waxed paper. Divide the crab mixture into 4 or 8 equal portions, and shape each portion into a cake about 3/4 inch (2 cm) thick. As each cake is formed, dip it in the bread crumbs, turning to coat completely, and then place it on the prepared baking sheet.

In a large frying pan over medium-high heat, add enough olive oil to film the bottom lightly. When hot, add the crab cakes, a few at a time, and fry, turning once, until golden brown, 3–4 minutes on each side.

Transfer to warmed individual plates and serve at once.

Serves 4

Honey-Cured Smoked Salmon

This home-smoked salmon fillet is delectably moist and sweet thanks to a honey-and-rum brine. A dry smoker is a must here. Serve it with thin slices of rye bread spread with sweet butter.

In a nonaluminum bowl or deep dish large enough to hold the salmon flat, combine the water, honey, rum, lemon juice, salt, cloves, peppercorns, allspice berries, and bay leaf. Stir to mix well. Add the salmon, skin side up. Cover and refrigerate for 2 hours.

Rinse the salmon under cold running water and pat dry with paper towels. Place on a rack and let air-dry in a cool spot for 1 hour.

Prepare a low-heat fire in a dry smoker according to manufacturers' directions.

Place the salmon, skin side down, on the highest rack. Cover and smoke, keeping the temperature between 150°F (65°C) and 170°F (77°C), until the salmon is firm to the touch, about 1 1/2 hours.

If serving warm, transfer to a cutting board and let stand for 5 minutes. Slice thinly across the grain and transfer to a serving platter. If serving chilled, cool, then cover and refrigerate for 2–6 hours before slicing. Garnish with the capers and lemon slices and serve.

Serves 6

4 cups (32 fl oz/1 l) water

3/4 cup (9 oz/280 g) honey

1/4 cup (2 fl oz/60 ml) golden rum

1/4 cup (2 fl oz/60 ml) lemon juice

1/2 cup (4 oz/125 g) salt

10 whole cloves

10 peppercorns

10 allspice berries

1 bay leaf

1 large salmon fillet with skin intact, 1 3/4–2 lb (875 g–1 kg)

1 tablespoon capers

Lemon slices

Confetti Crabmeat Soufflé Roll

FOR THE CRABMEAT FILLING

2 tablespoons unsalted butter

8 green (spring) onions, finely chopped

¼ cup (1½ oz/45 g) *each* minced fresh green chiles and red bell pepper (capsicum)

1 lb (500 g) cooked crabmeat

⅓ cup (½ oz/15 g) chopped fresh dill

1 tablespoon lemon juice

½ lb (250 g) cream cheese, at room temperature

About 1½ tablespoons heavy (double) cream

Salt and ground black pepper to taste

FOR THE SOUFFLÉ ROLL

¼ cup (2 oz/60 g) unsalted butter

½ cup (2½ oz/75 g) all-purpose (plain) flour

1 teaspoon salt, plus a pinch

2 cups (16 fl oz/500 ml) milk, heated almost to a boil

¼ teaspoon ground white pepper

Pinch of cayenne pepper

5 eggs, separated

6 tablespoons (1½ oz/45 g) grated Parmesan cheese

To make the filling, in a small sauté pan over medium heat, melt the butter. Add the onions, chiles, and bell pepper and sauté for 3 minutes. Stir in the crabmeat and sauté for 3 minutes longer. Stir in the dill and lemon juice. Remove from the heat. In a bowl, whisk together the cream cheese and enough cream to create a smooth mixture. Stir in the crab mixture. Season with salt and pepper. Cover and set aside.

Preheat an oven to 400°F (200°C). Butter a 15½-by-10½-by-1-inch (39-by-26.5-by-2.5-cm) jelly-roll (Swiss roll) pan. Line with parchment (baking) paper, butter the paper, dust with flour, and tap out the excess.

To make the soufflé roll, in a saucepan over medium-high heat, melt the butter. Stir in the flour and 1 teaspoon salt. Cook, stirring, for 2 minutes; do not brown. Remove from the heat and quickly whisk in the milk. Return to medium-high heat, bring to a boil, reduce the heat to medium, and cook, stirring, for 1 minute. Remove from the heat and stir in the white and cayenne peppers.

Place the egg yolks in a small bowl. Slowly whisk in about 1 cup (8 fl oz/250 ml) of the hot sauce, then whisk the yolk mixture back into the sauce. Set over medium heat and cook, stirring, for 1 minute. Do not allow to boil. Remove from the heat.

In a bowl, beat the egg whites with a pinch of salt until stiff peaks form. Fold the whites into the warm sauce until incorporated. Immediately spread the mixture in the prepared pan. Bake until puffed and golden, 25–30 minutes.

Meanwhile, lay a kitchen towel on a large cake rack and sprinkle evenly with 4 tablespoons of the Parmesan cheese. When the soufflé is done, immediately invert the pan onto the towel. Lift off the pan, peel off the paper, and spread the filling evenly on the soufflé. Using the towel and starting from a long side, roll up the soufflé. Using the towel as a cradle, transfer the roll, seam side down, to a serving platter. Sprinkle with the remaining cheese. Cut into slices before serving.

Serves 12

Camembert-Filled Artichoke Bottoms

Start a special dinner with these elegant appetizers. Brie may be substituted for the Camembert. If you like, save the leaves when preparing these artichokes. Steam the leaves for 10 minutes, then snack on them while you're making dinner.

1 lemon, halved

6 large artichokes

2 cups (16 fl oz/500 ml) vegetable broth

3 leeks, white part only, cut into 1-inch (2.5-cm) pieces

3 tablespoons heavy (double) cream

Salt and ground pepper to taste

6 oz (185 g) Camembert cheese, rind removed

2 tomatoes, peeled, seeded, and diced

1 1/2 teaspoons minced fresh tarragon

Fill a large bowl three-fourths full with water and squeeze in the juice of 1/2 lemon, then drop the lemon half into the water. Working with 1 artichoke at a time, cut off the stem even with the base and snap or cut off all the leaves. Trim away the tough outer layer around the base. As you work, rub the cut surfaces with the remaining lemon half, and then drop the trimmed artichoke into the lemon water.

In a saucepan over high heat, bring the broth to a boil. Add the leeks, reduce the heat to medium, and simmer, uncovered, until very tender, 15–20 minutes.

Meanwhile, preheat an oven to 325°F (165°C). Bring a separate saucepan three-fourths full of water to a boil. Drain the artichoke bottoms, add them to the boiling water, and cook until easily pierced, 12–15 minutes. Drain and, when cool enough to handle, gently scrape out and discard the choke from each artichoke bottom. Place the artichoke bottoms, stem ends down, on a lightly oiled baking sheet.

When the leeks are done, remove from the heat. Using a slotted spoon, transfer them to a blender or food processor. Add 2–3 tablespoons of the cooking liquid and the cream. Purée until smooth. Season with salt and pepper. Cover and keep warm.

Cut the Camembert cheese into 6 equal pieces. Put 1 piece on top of each artichoke bottom. Cover with aluminum foil and place in the oven until the cheese melts, 8–10 minutes. Remove from the oven.

Divide the leek purée among 6 warmed plates. Place an artichoke bottom on each plate. Sprinkle the tomato and tarragon around each artichoke and serve.

Serves 6

Parmesan Filo Napoleon

To keep the filo crisp, assemble the layers of this elegant first course just before serving. Since filo is often available frozen, make sure to thaw it before using. Leftover filo can be wrapped airtight with plastic wrap and refrigerated for up to 3 days.

Preheat an oven to 375°F (190°C). Line 2 baking sheets with parchment (baking) paper. Working with 1 filo sheet at a time and keeping the others covered with a damp kitchen towel to prevent drying, lay the sheet on a cutting board. Brush with the melted butter and sprinkle with about 2 tablespoons of the cheese. Repeat with 2 more filo sheets, stacking them on top of the first. Cut lengthwise into quarters, then cut crosswise into quarters, creating 16 rectangles. Place on a prepared baking sheet. Repeat with 3 more filo sheets and place on the second baking sheet. Bake until golden brown, 8–10 minutes. Let cool.

Meanwhile, in a small bowl, whisk together the vinegar, egg yolk, and mustard. While whisking constantly, drizzle in the $^{1}/_{2}$ cup (4 fl oz/125 ml) olive oil to form a vinaigrette. Season with salt and pepper. Set aside.

Bring a pot three-fourths full of water to a boil. Add the corn, blanch for 2 minutes. Drain, immerse in ice water, and drain again. Set aside. Refill the pot and blanch the potato slices for 30 seconds. Drain, immerse in ice water, and drain again. Pat dry.

In a sauté pan over medium heat, warm the remaining 3 tablespoons olive oil. Add the potatoes, season liberally with salt and pepper, and sauté until golden brown, 7–9 minutes. Using a slotted spoon, transfer to paper towels to drain briefly, then place in a bowl. Add the spinach and corn, drizzle on the vinaigrette, and toss well.

To assemble the napoleons, place 1 filo rectangle on each individual plate. Top with a spoonful of the potato-corn mixture. Repeat the layers twice, then top with with a filo rectangle. Serve at once.

Serves 8

6 filo sheets, thawed in the refrigerator if frozen

$^{1}/_{2}$ cup (4 oz/125 g) unsalted butter, melted

$^{3}/_{4}$ cup (3 oz/90 g) finely grated Parmesan cheese

2 teaspoons red wine vinegar

1 egg yolk

1 teaspoon Dijon mustard

$^{1}/_{2}$ cup (4 fl oz/125 ml) plus 3 tablespoons extra-virgin olive oil

Salt and ground pepper to taste

1 cup (6 oz/185 g) corn kernels

Ice water as needed

3 baking potatoes, peeled and thinly sliced

3 cups (3 oz/90 g) spinach leaves, shredded

Layered Vegetable Terrine with Mustard Vinaigrette

6 thin slices peeled Asian eggplant (aubergine)

2 red bell peppers (capsicums), halved lengthwise and seeded

2 fresh portobello mushrooms, brushed clean and sliced

1 yellow summer squash, cut lengthwise into 3 or 4 slices

$1/2$ cup (4 fl oz/125 ml) olive oil

2 cloves garlic, finely chopped

2 leeks, halved lengthwise

2 tablespoons water

$1/2$ lb (250 g) spinach

Salt and ground pepper to taste

$1/2$ cup ($1/2$ oz/15 g) loosely packed fresh basil leaves, torn into pieces

$1/4$ lb (125 g) mozzarella cheese, thinly sliced

FOR THE VINAIGRETTE

3 tablespoons red wine vinegar

1 tablespoon balsamic vinegar

1 clove garlic, finely chopped

1 teaspoon *each* Dijon mustard and dried thyme

Salt and ground pepper to taste

$2/3$ cup (5 fl oz/160 ml) olive oil

Preheat an oven to 400°F (200°C). Oil 2 large baking sheets. Arrange the eggplant and bell peppers on 1 baking sheet. Arrange the mushrooms and squash on the second baking sheet. In a small bowl, combine the oil and garlic and brush over the vegetables. Roast the mushrooms and squash until browned on the bottoms, about 15 minutes. Turn and roast 10 minutes longer. Meanwhile, roast the eggplant and peppers until browned, about 25 minutes. Turn and brown the other side, about 20 minutes longer. Remove all the vegetables from the oven. Transfer the peppers to a plate and drape with aluminum foil. Let cool, then peel. Let all the vegetables cool.

Meanwhile, arrange the leeks in a baking dish. Add the water and drizzle with a little of the remaining oil-garlic mixture. Cover tightly and bake until very tender, 25–30 minutes. Remove from the oven and let cool. Place the spinach on a steamer rack over simmering water, cover, and steam until wilted, about 2 minutes. Transfer to a sieve and press down to extract the moisture. Chop coarsely.

Reduce the oven temperature to 350°F (180°C). Lightly brush a 1$1/2$-qt (1.5-l) glass loaf dish with any remaining oil-garlic mixture. Sprinkle all of the vegetables with salt and pepper. Arrange the pepper halves in the bottom of the prepared dish, cut sides up. Arrange the squash slices on top in a single layer. Sprinkle with half of the torn basil, top with the spinach, and then with the cheese. Arrange the mushrooms in a layer, and top with the leeks. Sprinkle with the remaining basil. Top with the eggplant slices, slightly overlapping them. Cover with foil and press down to compact the vegetables. Bake until heated through, about 30 minutes. Remove from the oven but do not uncover. Let stand for about 30 minutes before serving.

To make the vinaigrette, in a bowl, whisk together the vinegars, garlic, mustard, thyme, salt, and pepper. Slowly whisk in the oil.

Unmold the terrine onto a cutting board. Cut into slices. Serve with the vinaigrette.

Serves 8

Chilled Mussels with Tomatoes and Sherry Vinegar

These mussels are the best when served icy cold, so prepare this dish well in advance. You can make this recipe with clams instead of mussels. Increase the amount to 4 pounds (2 kg) and steam them for 3–5 minutes.

Discard any mussels that fail to close to the touch. In a large frying pan over medium-high heat, bring the water to a boil. Add the mussels, cover, and cook just until most of the mussels open, 2–3 minutes. Uncover and, using tongs, transfer the opened mussels to a shallow bowl, allowing any liquid from the shells to drain back into the pan. Re-cover and continue to cook until all of the mussels have opened, 1 minute or so longer. Transfer the additional opened mussels to the bowl and discard any that failed to open. Let cool.

Meanwhile, return the pan to high heat and cook until the liquid is reduced to 2 tablespoons, about 3 minutes. Pour into a small bowl and let cool. The add the tomatoes, green onions, parsley, garlic, paprika, saffron threads, olive oil, and vinegar. Toss to mix well. Season with salt and pepper.

When the mussels are cool, remove the top shell from each mussel and discard. Place the mussels still in their bottom shells in a serving bowl. Add the tomato mixture and toss together. Cover and refrigerate for at least 2 hours or for up to 6 hours before serving.

Serves 6

1½ (750 g) mussels, well scrubbed and debearded

½ cup (4 fl oz/125 ml) water

2 tomatoes, peeled, seeded, and chopped

2 green (spring) onions, including tender green tops, thinly sliced

1 tablespoon chopped fresh flat-leaf (Italian) parsley

1 clove garlic, minced

½ teaspoon sweet paprika

Large pinch of saffron threads

2 tablespoons extra-virgin olive oil

1 tablespoon sherry vinegar

Salt and ground pepper to taste

Salads

Watercress, Pear, and Goat Cheese Salad with Sherry Vinaigrette

If preferred, a mix of young, tender salad greens can be used in place of the watercress, while Bosc pears can stand in for the Bartletts. And, if you like, a cow's milk cheese such as a mild Gorgonzola dolcelatte can replace the goat cheese.

Peel, halve, and core the pears, then cut each half into 4 wedges.

As the pears are cut, place them in a large bowl and sprinkle with the lemon juice. Add the watercress and cherries.

To make the vinaigrette, in a small bowl, whisk together the olive oil, sherry vinegar, salt, and pepper until blended.

Drizzle the vinaigrette over the watercress mixture, then toss to coat evenly. Divide the salad evenly among individual plates. Add the goat cheese to the salads, distributing it evenly. Serve immediately.

Serves 6

3 firm but ripe Bartlett (Williams') pears

Juice from 1/2 lemon

2 or 3 bunches watercress, long stems removed (about 8 cups/8 oz/250 g)

1/2 cup (2 oz/60 g) moist dried pitted sweet cherries

FOR THE VINAIGRETTE

6 tablespoons (3 fl oz/90 ml) extra-virgin olive oil

2 tablespoons sherry wine vinegar

1/2 teaspoon salt

Ground pepper to taste

5 oz (155 g) semi-firm mild-aged goat cheese, cut into small pieces

Arugula and Orange Salad with Pomegranate-White Wine Vinaigrette

To save time the day of serving, remove the seeds from the pomegranate up to 2 days in advance. Store in the refrigerator in an airtight container. Do not extract the juice until 1–2 hours before making the vinaigrette.

FOR THE VINAIGRETTE

1 pomegranate

$^1/_3$ cup (3 fl oz/80 ml) extra-virgin olive oil

2 tablespoons white wine vinegar or raspberry vinegar

1 teaspoon sugar

$^1/_2$ teaspoon salt

Ground pepper to taste

2 large navel oranges

3 bunches arugula (rocket), tough stems removed

1 small red (Spanish) onion, cut crosswise into thin rings

To make the vinaigrette, carefully remove the skin from the pomegranate. Working over a sieve placed over a bowl to catch the juices, peel away the thick membrane from the pomegranate seeds and allow the loosened seeds to collect in the sieve. Measure $^1/_3$ cup ($1\,^1/_2$ oz/45 g) of the seeds and reserve for garnish. Press on the remaining seeds with the back of a spoon to release about 2 tablespoons juice. Discard the crushed seeds.

Add the olive oil, vinegar, sugar, salt, and pepper to the pomegranate juice. Whisk until blended.

Using a small, sharp knife, cut a slice off the top and bottom of each orange to expose the flesh. Place each orange upright on a cutting board and thickly slice off the peel in strips, following the contour of the orange to expose the flesh. Holding the orange over a large bowl, cut along either side of each section, letting the section drop into the bowl. Add the arugula and red onion, separating the onion slices into rings. Drizzle the dressing over the arugula mixture, then toss to coat evenly.

Divide the salad among individual plates, distributing the orange sections evenly. Garnish with the reserved pomegranate seeds. Serve at once.

Serves 6

Celery Root and Carrot Salad with Creamy Dressing

This crisp, refreshing salad is best made a day ahead. Celery root darkens quickly once the flesh is exposed to air. To discourage discoloring, immerse cut celery root in a bowl of water mixed with a little vinegar until ready to coat with the dressing.

To make the dressing, in a large nonaluminum bowl, combine the olive oil, cream, mustard, vinegar, salt, and pepper. Whisk until blended.

Using a sharp knife, peel away the tough skin from the celery root. Using a mandoline or the knife, cut into thin julienne strips about 3 inches (7.5 cm) long. Immediately add to the dressing and turn to coat well. Work quickly, as the flesh begins to discolor as soon as it is exposed to the air. Add the shredded carrot and mix well. Cover and refrigerate for at least 1 hour or for as long as overnight before serving. (If the salad becomes very cold, let stand at room temperature for 15 minutes before serving.)

To serve, arrange a lettuce leaf on each individual plate. Divide the celery root mixture evenly among the leaves. Sprinkle each salad with a few capers. Garnish with tarragon sprigs, if using. Serve at once.

Serves 6

FOR THE DRESSING

1/2 cup (4 fl oz/125 ml) pure olive oil or 2 tablespoons pure olive oil and 6 tablespoons (3 fl oz/90 ml) extra-virgin olive oil

1/4 cup (2 fl oz/60 ml) heavy (double) cream

2 tablespoons Dijon mustard

2 tablespoons tarragon vinegar

3/4 teaspoon salt

Ground pepper to taste

1 large celery root, about 1 1/2 lb (750 g)

1/2 cup (2 oz/60 g) coarsely shredded carrot

6 large butter (Boston) lettuce leaves

1 tablespoon capers, rinsed and well drained

Fresh tarragon sprigs (optional)

Begian Endive, Celery Root, and Pear Salad

This rich salad is an excellent beginning to a holiday meal. Select Bosc or Anjou pears that are ripe, yet still firm to the touch. Once you have grated the celery root, toss it with the vinaigrette to keep it from turning brown.

½ cup (2½ oz/75 g) hazelnuts (filberts)

2 tablespoons sherry wine vinegar

1 shallot, minced

½ cup (4 fl oz/125 ml) hazelnut oil or vegetable oil

Salt and ground pepper to taste

5 heads Belgian endive (chicory/witloof)

1 celery root (celeriac), peeled and coarsely grated

1 head radicchio, shredded

2 pears (see note)

1 lemon, halved

Preheat an oven to 350°F (180°C). Spread the hazelnuts on a baking sheet and toast until fragrant and the skins have loosened, 5–7 minutes. While still warm, transfer to a kitchen towel. Rub the towel vigorously to remove the skins; do not worry if small bits remain. Coarsely chop and set aside.

In a bowl, combine the vinegar and shallot. While whisking continuously, slowly drizzle in the hazelnut or vegetable oil to form a vinaigrette. Season with salt and pepper. Set aside.

Separate the leaves from the Belgian endive. Cut them lengthwise into long, narrow strips and place in a bowl. Add the celery root, radicchio, and all but 2 tablespoons of the vinaigrette. Toss to coat evenly, then divide among chilled individual plates.

Peel, halve, and core each pear, leaving the stems intact, if desired. Place each half, flat side down, on a cutting board and cut lengthwise into thin slices, leaving the slices attached at the stem end. Rub the cut surfaces with the lemon halves to prevent browning, then fan each pear half atop a mound of greens. Drizzle evenly with the reserved vinaigrette, sprinkle with the hazelnuts, and serve.

Serves 4

Fingerling Potato Salad with Shrimp and Baby Dill

Fingerling potatoes have the elongated, narrow shape of a finger. Generally thin-skinned with waxy, firm flesh, they are excellent boiling potatoes and ideal for making potato salads.

In a large saucepan, combine the potatoes with water to cover by 2 inches (5 cm). Add 1 teaspoon of the salt and bring to a boil over high heat. Reduce the heat to medium and cook until the potatoes are tender when pierced with a sharp knife, 20–25 minutes.

Drain the potatoes and, as soon as they are cool enough to handle, peel and cut crosswise into slices $1/4$ inch (6 mm) thick. Put the slices in a bowl and add the yogurt, sour cream, and mayonnaise. Turn gently to coat evenly. Add all but 4 of the shrimp, the green onion, chopped dill, pepper, and the remaining $1/2$ teaspoon salt and turn again to mix well. Cover and refrigerate for at least 6 hours or up to 24 hours to allow the flavors to blend fully. Cover and refrigerate the reserved shrimp as well.

To serve, top the salad with the reserved shrimp and a sprig or two of dill. Serve well chilled.

Serves 4

2½ lb (1.25 kg) fingerling potatoes such as Ruby Crescent, Lady Finger, or Ratte (La Rote), unpeeled

1½ teaspoons salt

½ cup (4 oz/125 g) plain yogurt

½ cup (4 fl oz/125 ml) light sour cream

2 tablespoons mayonnaise

½ lb (250 g) cooked bay shrimp

¾ cup (2 oz/60 g) chopped green (spring) onion

½ cup (¾ oz/20 g) chopped baby dill, plus 1 or 2 sprigs for garnish

1 teaspoon ground pepper

Fresh Cranberry Beans, Broccoli Rabe, and Pancetta Salad

The delightfully bitter taste of broccoli rabe provides an appealing counterpoint to the soft, sweet taste of the cranberry beans in this delicious salad. Broccoli rabe is at its peak of flavor when you can see some yellow in the buds and a few flowers are open.

1¹/₂–2 lb (750 g–1 kg) fresh cranberry (borlotti) beans or other fresh shelling beans

³/₄ teaspoon salt

1 bay leaf

2 fresh winter savory or thyme sprigs

1 lb (500 g) broccoli rabe

¹/₃ cup (3 fl oz/80 ml) extra-virgin olive oil

2 cloves garlic, minced

¹/₂ teaspoon ground pepper

¹/₂ lb (125 g) pancetta, thinly sliced and cut into 1-inch (2.5-cm) pieces

3–4 tablespoons red wine vinegar

Shell the beans; you should have about 1 cup (6 oz/185 g). Place them in a saucepan with water to cover by 2 inches (5 cm). Add ¹/₂ teaspoon of the salt, the bay leaf, and the winter savory or thyme and bring to a boil over high heat. Reduce the heat to medium and cook, uncovered, until tender, 15–25 minutes. The cooking time will depend upon the maturity of the beans; older beans will take longer to cook.

Meanwhile, remove any tough stems from the broccoli rabe and discard. Chop the tender portions; you should have about 2 cups (6 oz/185 g). When the beans are almost done, in a frying pan over medium-high heat, warm the olive oil. When it is hot, add the garlic and sauté until translucent, 2–3 minutes. Add the broccoli rabe and sprinkle with the remaining ¹/₄ teaspoon salt and the pepper. Cook, stirring often, until the greens change color and are tender to the bite, 4–5 minutes. Remove from the heat and cover to keep warm. Set aside.

At the same time, in a small frying pan, cook the pancetta until the fat is translucent, 3–4 minutes.

Drain the beans and place in a warmed serving bowl. Add the broccoli rabe and the pancetta with any of its rendered fat. Then add the vinegar to taste and toss to mix well. Serve immediately.

Serves 4

Mixed Greens with Caramelized Pears and Pecans

A crisp, green salad makes a nice addition to any menu. This one—featuring sautéed pears and pecans—is especially nice during the autumn and winter months. Use prepackaged mixed greens, or use a mix of any of your favorites.

Put the greens into a large salad bowl and crumble the goat cheese over the top. Cover the bowl with plastic wrap and refrigerate until ready to serve.

Just before serving, make the dressing: In a small bowl, combine the vinegar, olive oil, mustard, salt, and pepper in the small bowl. Beat with the fork until blended. Set aside.

With a small, sharp knife, peel and core the pears, then cut each pear lengthwise into eighths.

In a large, nonstick frying pan over medium heat, melt the butter. Add the pear wedges and sauté for 1 minute, gently turning the pears with a spatula to coat them with butter. Sprinkle the sugar over the pears. Continue to cook, turning occasionally, for 2 minutes. Add the pecans and continue to cook, stirring gently and turning the pears, until the pears are beginning to brown and the pecans are heated through, about 3 minutes.

Remove the greens from the refrigerator. Stir the dressing with the fork, pour over the greens, and toss gently to mix. Spoon on the pear mixture and toss again. Serve immediately.

Serves 6

8 cups (about 1/2 lb/250 g) mixed torn salad greens

3 oz (90 g) fresh goat cheese

1 tablespoon red wine vinegar

3 tablespoons olive oil

1/2 teaspoon Dijon mustard

1/4 teaspoon salt

1/8 teaspoon pepper

3 ripe pears

3 tablespoons unsalted butter

1 1/2 tablespoons granulated sugar

1/2 cup (2 oz/60 g) pecan halves

Soups

Seafood Bisque

This rich bisque, thick with lobster, shrimp, and bay scallops, should be served in small wamed bowls or cups. You can make this soup up to two days in advance and reheat, stirring gently, over low heat. Garnish each one with a small sprig of tarragon.

8 cups (64 fl oz/2 l) water

2 fresh thyme sprigs
or 1 teaspoon dried thyme

2 fresh tarragon sprigs
or 1 teaspoon dried tarragon

1 large sweet onion such as
Vidalia, halved

1 bay leaf

1 leafy celery stalk top

1 teaspoon salt, plus salt to
taste

1 live lobster, about 1¹/₂ lb
(750 g)

¹/₂ lb (250 g) large shrimp
(prawns) in the shell

¹/₄ cup (2 oz/60 g) unsalted
butter, at room temperature

¹/₄ cup (1¹/₂ oz/ 45 g) all-
purpose (plain) flour

2 cups (16 fl oz/500 ml) heavy
(double) cream

1 tablespoon tomato paste

Ground white pepper to taste

¹/₂ lb (250 g) bay scallops

In a large saucepan over medium heat, combine the water, thyme, tarragon, onion, bay leaf, celery top, and 1 teaspoon salt. Bring to a boil, cover, reduce the heat to low, and simmer for 10 minutes. Uncover and return to a boil over high heat. Add the lobster, cover, reduce the heat to medium-high, and cook for 8 minutes. Uncover, add the shrimp, re-cover, and cook until the shrimp turn pink, about 4 minutes. Using tongs, transfer the lobster to a platter to cool. Strain the contents of the saucepan into a large bowl. Return the broth to the saucepan. Place the shrimp on the platter with the lobster. Discard the other solids.

Lay the cooled lobster, right side up, on a cutting board. Insert a knife where the body meets the tail and cut the tail in half lengthwise. Turn the lobster and cut toward the head, cutting the lobster into 2 pieces. Discard the organs. Remove all the meat from the body. Using a mallet, crack the claws and remove the meat. Peel the shrimp. Work over the platter as much as possible to save the juices and the shells. Cut the lobster and shrimp into ¹/₂-inch (12-mm) pieces. Set aside. Return the shells and juices to the broth, bring to a simmer, cover, reduce the heat to low, and cook until fragrant, about 30 minutes. Let cool slightly, then strain into a bowl.

In a saucepan over medium heat, melt the butter. Stir in the flour and cook, stirring, for 3 minutes. Whisk in the broth and bring to a boil. Reduce the heat to low and whisk in the cream. Stir in the tomato paste, salt, white pepper, and the reserved lobster and shrimp. Add the scallops and cook, stirring, until opaque, about 1 minute. Taste and adjust the seasonings. Ladle into warmed bowls and serve.

Serves 6

Tomato Soup with Minted Goat Cheese

This deep red tomato soup looks far more complicated to assemble than its simple preparation proves. It is best when made a day ahead and reheated. Make the garnish ahead too. Just refrigerate and bring to room temperature before serving.

In a large, deep-sided nonaluminum saucepan over medium heat, warm the olive oil. When hot, add the onion and carrot and sauté, stirring, until beginning to soften, about 3 minutes. Add the garlic and sauté, stirring, for 1 minute longer. Add the tomatoes, 3 1/2 cups (28 fl oz/875 ml) broth, salt, and cayenne pepper. Bring to a simmer, reduce the heat to low, and simmer, uncovered, until all the vegetables are tender, 30–35 minutes.

Remove from the heat and let cool for 10 minutes. Working in batches, purée in the food processor or blender until smooth. Return the soup to the saucepan over medium heat and heat to serving temperature, about 5 minutes. If the soup is too thick, thin with the remaining 1/2 cup (4 fl oz/125 ml) broth. Taste and adjust the seasonings.

To make the garnish, place the cheese in a small nonaluminum bowl. Whisk in the milk, 1 tablespoon at a time, until the mixture is smooth and the consistency of a medium-thick sauce. You may not need all of the milk.

To serve, ladle the soup into warmed bowls. Drizzle each serving with about 3 tablespoons of the goat cheese, forming a zig zag pattern. Garnish each serving with 1 teaspoon mint.

Serves 4

3 tablespoons olive oil

2 cups (10 oz/315 g) chopped yellow onion

1 cup (5 oz/155 g) peeled and diced carrot

1 tablespoon chopped garlic

2 cans (28 oz/875 g each) plum (Roma) tomatoes, drained well and coarsely chopped

3 1/2–4 cups (28–32 fl oz/875 ml–1 l) chicken broth

1 teaspoon salt

1/8 teaspoon cayenne pepper

FOR THE GOAT CHEESE GARNISH

5 oz (155 g) creamy fresh goat cheese

2–3 tablespoons milk

4 teaspoons chopped fresh mint

Matzo Ball Soup

Although traditionally made for Passover, matzo ball soup is a heart-warming soup any time of the year. To this simple version, you may also add diced cooked chicken and/or carrots, as well as English peas and a sprinkling of parsley, if you like.

2 eggs

3 tablespoons vegetable oil

1 tablespoon water

½ cup (2 oz/60 g) matzo meal

1 teaspoon salt

8 cups (64 fl oz/2 l) chicken broth

In a small bow, combine the eggs, oil, and water. Beat with the fork until well blended. Add the matzo meal and salt and stir until combined. Cover and refrigerate until firm, about 30 minutes.

Bring a large pot three-fourths full of water to a gentle boil over medium-high heat. Using wet hands, form the matzo-meal mixture into 6 equal-sized balls. Then, using a slotted spoon, gently slip the balls into the boiling water. Cover and cook for 35 minutes.

Meanwhile, bring the broth to a gentle boil in a saucepan over medium heat. Reduce the heat and simmer until the matzo balls are done.

When the matzo balls are cooked, ladle the broth into the 6 soup bowls, dividing it evenly. With the slotted spoon, transfer 1 matzo ball to each bowl. Serve immediately.

Serves 6

Caramelized Red Onion Soup with Goat Cheese Crostini

Long cooking intensifies the natural sweetness of the onions and deepens the flavor of this soup—a contemporary interpretation of the French bistro classic. Just a little bit of goat cheese goes a long way toward enriching this light soup.

Heat a heavy saucepan over medium heat. Coat the pan with nonstick cooking spray. Add the onions, garlic, sugar, and thyme, and season with salt and pepper. Cook, stirring often, until the onions are quite soft but haven't begun to color, about 25 minutes.

Pour in the wine and deglaze the pan, stirring with a wooden spoon to remove any browned bits from the pan bottom. Simmer over medium heat until the liquid has evaporated, about 15 minutes.

Add the broth and simmer over medium heat until reduced to about 4 cups (32 fl oz/1 l), about 10 minutes. Meanwhile, spread the goat cheese on the toasted bread slices.

Ladle the soup into warmed bowls. Float 2 toasts in each bowl. Garnish the toasts with thyme sprigs, if desired. Serve hot.

Serves 4

3 red (Spanish) onions, thinly sliced

4 cloves garlic, thinly sliced

2 teaspoons brown sugar

1 teaspoon dried thyme

Salt and ground pepper to taste

1 cup (8 fl oz/250 ml) dry red wine

3 cups (24 fl oz/750 ml) chicken broth

1/4 cup (2 oz/60 g) herb-flavored soft goat cheese

8 slices baguette, each about 1/2 inch (12 mm) thick, toasted

Fresh thyme sprigs (optional)

Gazpacho

This delightful soup makes a refreshing counterpoint to many richer offerings. Set out a big bowl of the soup nestled in a larger bowl of ice and let guests help themselves. Arrange smaller bowls of garnishes alongside for sprinkling on top.

Ice water, as needed

6–8 large beefsteak or other full-flavored tomatoes

1 small sweet yellow or red (Spanish) onion, chopped

4 cloves garlic

6 tablespoons (3 fl oz/90 ml) red wine vinegar, or to taste

2 regular or 1 English (hothouse) cucumber, halved, peeled, seeded, and diced

1/2 cup (4 fl oz/125 ml) extra-virgin olive oil, plus 2 tablespoons for frying croutons

Salt and ground pepper to taste

3 or 4 thick (1-inch/2.5-cm) slices French or Italian bread, crusts removed and cut into 1-inch (2.5-cm) cubes

1 small green bell pepper (capsicum), seeded and finely diced

1/4 cup (1 1/4 oz/37 g) finely minced red (Spanish) onion

Bring a large saucepan three-fourths full of water to a boil. Have ready a large bowl of ice water. Meanwhile, cut a shallow cross on the blossom end of each tomato, and then remove the core. Blanch the tomatoes in the boiling water for 30 seconds, then, using a slotted spoon, transfer to the ice water to cool. Remove from the water and peel immediately. Cut the tomatoes in half crosswise and squeeze out the seeds. In a blender or food processor, purée 3 of the tomatoes until liquefied and transfer to a large bowl. Reserve the remaining tomatoes.

Put the onion in the blender or food processor. Chop 3 of the garlic cloves and add them as well. Purée, adding a bit of the vinegar if needed for a smooth consistency. Add to the bowl holding the tomato purée. Add the cucumbers to the blender or processor and pulse to chop coarsely. Add to the bowl as well. Chop the remaining tomatoes coarsely in the blender or processor. Add to the bowl. Whisk in the 1/2 cup (4 fl oz/125 ml) olive oil and the remaining vinegar. Season with salt and pepper. Serve, or cover and refrigerate until well chilled, about 2 hours.

Just before serving the soup, in a large frying pan over medium heat, warm the 2 tablespoons olive oil. Crush the remaining garlic clove, add to the pan, and cook for a minute or two to release its fragrance. Add the bread cubes and stir and toss until golden brown, about 5 minutes. Transfer to paper towels to drain; keep warm.

Taste the soup and adjust the seasonings with salt. Ladle into chilled bowls and garnish each serving with the diced bell pepper and the minced onion. Float the croutons on top and serve.

Serves 6–8

Mussel Bisque with Saffron

This creamy bisque is an ideal prelude to a special dinner. If your mussels have been purchased with the beards attached, just scrub the shells well and cook them with the beards, then remove the beards when the shells have opened.

Discard any mussels that do not close to the touch. In a large, wide pan over high heat, combine the mussels and wine. Cover and cook, shaking the pan from time to time, until the mussels open, about 5 minutes. Remove from the heat and, when the mussels are cool enough to handle, discard any that did not open. Remove the remainder from their shells, picking off and discarding the beards and the shells. Pour the liquid through a sieve lined with damp cheesecloth (muslin) placed over a large bowl. Add water or fish stock as needed to measure about 6 cups (48 fl oz/1.5 l). Cover the cooked mussels with about 1 cup (8 fl oz/250 ml) of the cooking liquid and refrigerate.

In a saucepan over medium heat, melt the butter. Add the leek or onion and the fennel, if using, and sauté, stirring occasionally, until softened, 8–10 minutes. Add the tomatoes, potato, saffron and sherry, orange zest, and the remaining 5 cups (40 fl oz/1.25 l) cooking liquid. Raise the heat to high and bring to a boil. Reduce the heat to low and simmer until the potato is soft, about 20 minutes.

Select 18–24 perfect mussels for garnish and add the rest to the soup, along with the liquid in the bowl. Working in batches, purée the soup in a blender. Strain through a fine-mesh sieve placed over a saucepan. Add the cream and reheat very gently over very low heat, about 5 minutes. Season with salt and pepper.

Ladle into warmed bowls. Garnish with the reserved whole mussels and the parsley and serve immediately.

Serves 6

5 lb (2.5 kg) mussels, well scrubbed

2 cups (16 fl oz/500 ml) dry white wine

About 4 cups (32 fl oz/1 l) water or fish stock

1/4 cup (2 oz/60 g) unsalted butter

1 cup (4 oz/125 g) chopped leek or yellow onion

1/2 cup (2 oz/60 g) chopped fennel (optional)

1 cup (6 oz/185 g) peeled, seeded, and chopped tomatoes (fresh or canned)

2 cups (10 oz/315 g) peeled and diced red potato

1 teaspoon saffron threads, steeped in 1/4 cup (2 fl oz/60 ml) dry sherry

1 orange zest strip

1 1/2 cups (12 fl oz/375 ml) heavy (double) cream, heated

Salt and ground pepper to taste

3 tablespoons chopped fresh flat-leaf (Italian) parsley

Roasted Butternut Squash Soup

This nutty soup makes a wonderful introduction to the Thanksgiving meal or as part of a cozy supper throughout the winter months. Roasting the squash makes it easier to peel and seed, and deepens its flavor, making for a wonderfully rich soup.

2 large butternut squashes, 1½–2 lb (750 g–1 kg) each

⅓ cup (2 oz/60 g) hazelnuts (filberts)

6 tablespoons (3 oz/90 g) unsalted butter

2 yellow onions, chopped

8 fresh sage leaves, shredded

6 cups (48 fl oz/1.5 l) chicken or vegetable broth

Salt and ground pepper to taste

Ground nutmeg to taste, if needed

Pinch of sugar, if needed

Preheat an oven to 400°F (200°C).

Prick each squash with the tip of a knife and place the whole squashes on a baking sheet. Roast until a knife penetrates the skin easily, about 1 hour. Remove from the oven and, when cool enough to handle, cut in half lengthwise and remove and discard the seeds and fibers. Scoop out the pulp into a bowl and set aside.

While the squashes are cooling, reduce the oven temperature to 350°F (180°C). Spread the hazelnuts on a baking sheet and toast until fragrant and the skins have loosened, about 10 minutes. Remove from the oven and, while still warm, place the nuts in a kitchen towel. Rub the towel vigorously to remove the skins; do not worry if small bits of skin remain. Chop and set aside.

In a saucepan over low heat, melt the butter. Add the onions and half of the sage and cook, stirring occasionally, until the onions are tender, 8–10 minutes. Add the broth and squash pulp and bring to a boil over high heat. Reduce the heat to low and simmer for a few minutes to combine the flavors. Remove from the heat.

Working in batches, purée the soup in a blender or food processor. Return to a clean saucepan. Reheat gently over medium-low heat. Season with salt and pepper. If the squash is starchy rather than sweet, a little nutmeg will help. If the nutmeg doesn't give the proper flavor balance, add a pinch of sugar.

Ladle into warmed bowls and garnish with the hazelnuts and the remaining sage. Serve at once.

Serves 6

Autumn Chicken Stew with Chanterelles

Using a serrated knife, cut off the top 3–4 inches (7.5–10 cm) from the stem end of the pumpkin. Using a spoon, scrape out the seeds and fibers. Using a melon baller, scoop out the flesh and set aside.

Dust the chicken pieces evenly with the paprika. In a dutch oven or other large pot over high heat, warm the oil. Add the chicken in batches and saute, turning once, until browned, about 2 minutes on each side. Transfer to a plate and season with salt and pepper, and set aside. Reduce the heat to medium and add the sausages. Cook until browned on all sides, about 4 minutes total. Transfer to a cutting board and, when cool enough to handle, slice into rounds $^1/_2$ inch (12 mm) thick.

In the same pot over medium high heat, add the carrots, garlic, onion, and bell pepper and sauté until softened, about 4 minutes. Stir in the flour and cook for 1 minute, stirring constantly. Raise the heat to high, pour in the stock and deglaze the pot, stirring to remove any browned bits from the bottom. The pour in the wine and add the reserved pumpkin, the potatoes, and thyme and marjoram to taste. Return the chicken and sausage to the pot, season with salt and pepper, and bring to a boil. Add half of the mushrooms. Reduce the heat to medium low, cover partially, and simmer until the chicken is opaque throughout and the juices run clear and the potatoes are tender, about 20 minutes. Stir in the remaining mushrooms and cook until tender, 5–10 minutes longer.

Transfer the stew to a large serving dish. Sprinkle with the parsley and serve.

Serves 6–8

1 pumpkin (4–6 lb/2–3 kg)

4 chicken breast halves, about $^1/_2$ lb (250 g) each, skinned

4 chicken thighs, about 6 oz (185 g) each, skinned

4 chicken drumsticks, about $^1/_4$ lb (125 g) each, skinned

1 lb (500 g) chicken wings

1 tablespoon paprika

2 tablespoons olive oil

Salt and ground pepper to taste

$^1/_2$ lb (250 g) Italian sausages

10–12 baby carrots, peeled

4 cloves garlic, slivered

1 yellow onion, chopped

1 red bell pepper (capsicum), seeded and chopped

2 tablespoons all-purpose (plain) flour

$1^1/_2$ cups (12 fl oz/375 ml) chicken broth

$1^1/_2$ cups (12 fl oz/375 m) dry white wine

8–12 small red potatoes

1–2 teaspoons *each* dried thyme and dried marjoram

$^1/_2$ lb (250 g) fresh chanterelle mushrooms, brushed clean and sliced

$^1/_2$ cup ($^3/_4$ oz/20 g) chopped fresh flat-leaf (Italian) parsley

Acorn Squash and Sweet Potato Soup with Walnut-Parsley Pesto

Your guests will be impressed when you serve this bright orange soup garnished with an emerald green swirl of parsley pesto. Roasting the acorn squashes and sweet potatoes offers an especially rich taste.

1 large sweet onion such as Vidalia, halved and sliced

4 cloves garlic, chopped

2 tablespoons unsalted butter,

1½ teaspoons salt, plus salt to taste

freshly ground pepper to taste

2 acorn squashes, about 2 lb (1 kg) each, halved lengthwise and seeds and fibers removed

2 sweet potatoes, about 1½ lb (750 g) total weight, peeled and sliced

FOR THE PESTO

½ cup (2 oz/60 g) walnuts

1 cup (1 oz/30 g) loosely packed fresh flat-leaf (Italian) parsley

1 clove garlic, coarsely chopped

½ teaspoon salt

⅔ cup (5 fl oz/160 ml) olive oil

¼ cup (1 oz/30 g) grated Parmesan cheese

4 cups (32 fl oz/1 l) chicken broth

1½ cups (12 fl oz/375 ml) half-and-half (half cream)

Preheat an oven to 400°F (200°C). Spread the onion slices and garlic in a large roasting pan. Cut the butter into pieces and sprinkle over the top. Sprinkle with ½ teaspoon of the salt and a grinding of pepper. Place the squashes and sweet potatoes, cut sides down, on top. Cover with aluminum foil. Bake until tender, about 1 hour. Uncover and let cool.

To make the pesto, reduce the oven temperature to 350°F (180°C). Spread the walnuts on a baking sheet and bake until golden, about 15 minutes. Remove from the oven and let cool slightly. In a food processor, combine the toasted walnuts, parsley, garlic, and salt. Process until finely chopped. With the motor running, add the olive oil in a slow, steady stream, processing until smooth and thick. Add the Parmesan and process until blended. You should have about ¾ cup (6 fl oz/180 ml).

Scoop the squash pulp into a food processor fitted with the metal blade. Add the sweet potatoes, onion, garlic, and any juices in the roasting pan. Puree the vegetables and transfer to a large saucepan. Add the broth and half-and-half and place over low heat. Bring to a gentle simmer, stirring occasionally. Add the remaining 1 teaspoon salt and season to taste with pepper. Do not allow to boil or the cream may curdle.

Ladle the soup into warmed shallow bowls. Swirl 1½ teaspoons pesto on each serving. Serve at once. Pass any remaining pesto at the table.

Serves 6–8

Barley and Root Vegetable Stew

Jerusalem artichokes, sometimes called sunchokes, are a tuberous vegetable with a flavor similar to artichokes. If you have trouble finding them, add an additional potato or favorite root vegetable in their place.

Preheat an oven to 400°F (200°C). Lightly oil a baking sheet.

In a large, heavy saucepan over medium-high heat, warm 3 tablespoons of the olive oil. Add the yellow onion, carrot, and celery and sauté until browned, 7–8 minutes. Raise the heat to high, add the wine, and deglaze the pan, stirring with a wooden spoon to dislodge any browned bits from the pan bottom. Continue to cook until the wine is reduced by one-half, about 5 minutes.

Add the broth and bring to a boil over high heat. Add the barley, parsley, and thyme and reduce the heat to medium-low. Cook, uncovered, for 35 minutes. Add the celery root, Jerusalem artichokes, and parsnips. Cover and cook over medium-low heat until tender, 15–20 minutes longer.

Meanwhile, in a large bowl, combine the red onion, potato, and the remaining 3 tablespoons olive oil. Toss to coat well. Spread on the prepared baking sheet and sprinkle with the sea salt. Roast until the vegetables are browned and tender, 40–45 minutes.

Add the roasted vegetables to the stockpot and stir well. Season with salt and pepper. Ladle into warmed bowls to serve.

Serves 6

6 tablespoons (3 fl oz/90 ml) extra-virgin olive oil

1 *each* yellow onion, carrot, and celery stalk, finely chopped

1 cup (8 fl oz/250 ml) dry white wine

5 1/2 cups (44 fl oz/1.3 l) vegetable broth

1/2 cup (4 oz/125 g) pearl barley

1/4 cup (1/3 oz/10 g) minced fresh flat-leaf (Italian) parsley

2 teaspoons minced fresh thyme

1 celery root (celeriac), peeled and diced

1/2 lb (250 g) Jerusalem artichokes, peeled and quartered (see note)

3 parsnips, peeled and thinly sliced crosswise

1 red (Spanish) onion, cut into 1-inch (2.5-cm) pieces

1 potato, unpeeled, cut into 1-inch (2.5-cm) pieces

2 teaspoons coarse sea salt

Salt and ground pepper to taste

Roast Turkey Vegetable Soup with Rice

Leftover soups like this one can be the best part of holiday cooking. Remove and set aside any remaining turkey meat that's clinging to the bones, then use the carcass to make the stock. Top each serving with chopped parsley and grated Parmesan.

TURKEY STOCK

Carcass from roast turkey

3–3$\frac{1}{2}$ qt (3–3.5 l) water

1 large yellow onion, chopped

2 carrots, peeled and chopped

1 celery stalk, chopped

4 fresh parsley sprigs

3 fresh thyme sprigs

1 bay leaf

5 tablespoons (2$\frac{1}{2}$ fl oz/75 ml) olive oil

1 yellow onion, chopped

3 carrots, peeled and diced

3 celery stalks, diced

$\frac{2}{3}$ cup (4$\frac{1}{2}$ oz/140 g) long-grain white rice

2 cups (6 oz/185 g) sliced fresh mushrooms

2 cups (4 oz/125 g) broccoli florets

2 cups (12 oz/375 g) diced cooked turkey

2 teaspoons chopped fresh thyme

Salt and ground pepper to taste

To make the stock, with your hands, break the carcass into big pieces and place them in a large stockpot with water to cover. Bring to a boil, skimming off any foam that forms on the surface. Reduce the heat to low, cover, and simmer for 1 hour, skimming as needed. Add the onion, carrots, celery, herb sprigs, and bay leaf. Cover partially and continue to simmer for about 1$\frac{1}{2}$ hours longer. Line a fine-mesh sieve with damp cheesecloth (muslin) and strain the stock into a large saucepan, and return to high heat. Bring to a boil, adjust the heat to maintain a gentle boil, and cook uncovered, skimming if needed, until reduced to about 8 cups (64 fl oz/2 l), about 1 hour. Remove from the heat and refrigerate, uncovered, until chilled, about 6 hours, then lift off and discard the fat solidified on top.

In a large saucepan over medium heat, warm 2 tablespoons of the olive oil. Add the onion, carrot, and celery and sauté, stirring often, until the onion is tender and translucent, about 10 minutes. Add the rice and stock and bring to a boil. Reduce the heat to low and simmer until the rice is tender, about 15 minutes.

Meanwhile, in a sauté pan over medium-high heat, warm the remaining 3 tablespoons oil. Add the mushrooms and sauté, stirring often, until tender, 8–10 minutes. Set aside. Bring a saucepan three-fourths full of lightly salted water to a boil, add the broccoli florets, and cook until tender but not falling apart, about 5 minutes. Drain, immerse in cold water, and drain again. Add the broccoli to the stock mixture along with the turkey, mushrooms, and thyme. Cook for 10 minutes. Season with salt and pepper, then ladle into warmed bowls and serve.

Serves 6–8

Vegetarian Cassoulet

Pick over the beans and discard any damaged beans or impurities. Rinse the beans. Place in a bowl, add water to cover generously, and let soak for about 3 hours.

In a saucepan over medium heat, warm 3 tablespoons of the olive oil. Add the onion, carrot, and celery and sauté until lightly browned, 5–7 minutes. Add the broth and bring to a boil over high heat. Drain the beans and add them to the pan. Gather the thyme sprig, parsley sprig, bay leaf, and celery leaves into a bundle and tie securely with kitchen string. Add to the pan along with the minced garlic. Reduce the heat to low, cover, and simmer until the beans are tender, about 1 1/2 hours. Discard the herb bundle.

Meanwhile, preheat an oven to 400°F (200°C). Lightly oil a large baking dish. In a bowl, combine the potatoes, red onion, and the remaining 3 tablespoons olive oil. Toss to coat. Spread in the prepared baking dish and sprinkle with the sea salt. Bake until lightly browned, about 45 minutes. Add the mushrooms and whole garlic cloves. Continue baking until the vegetables are browned, about 15 minutes longer.

Remove from the oven, transfer the vegetables to a plate, and set aside. Place the baking dish on the stove top over medium heat. Pour in the white wine and deglaze the dish, stirring with a wooden spoon to dislodge any browned bits from the dish bottom. Continue to cook until the wine is almost evaporated, 5–7 minutes. Add the cooked beans and their liquid, the roasted vegetables, minced thyme, and sun-dried tomatoes. Season with salt and pepper. Continue to cook until the vegetables are tender, 15–20 minutes. Serve at once.

Serves 6

1 cup (7 oz/220 g) dried small white beans

6 tablespoons (3 fl oz/90 ml) extra-virgin olive oil

1 yellow onion, chopped

1 carrot, peeled and chopped

1 celery stalk with leaves, chopped, leaves reserved

4 cups (32 fl oz/1 l) vegetable broth

1 *each* fresh thyme sprig, parsley sprig, and bay leaf

2 cloves garlic, minced, plus 10 whole cloves garlic

1 lb (500 g) red potatoes, unpeeled and diced

1 red (Spanish) onion, diced

1 tablespoon coarse sea salt

1/2 lb (250 g) fresh portobello mushrooms, cut into chunks

1 cup (8 fl oz/250 ml) white wine

1 teaspoon minced fresh thyme

1/2 cup (2 1/2 oz/75 g) drained, oil-packed sun-dried tomatoes

Salt and ground pepper to taste

Three-Mushroom Chowder

Add a wonderful splash of color and a punch of flavor to this earthy chowder by puréeing some roasted red pepper with a bit of cream, tomato paste, salt and a dash of cayenne pepper, then drizzling the purée over the top of each serving.

2 cups (16 fl oz/500 ml) reduced-sodium chicken broth

1/2 cup (1 oz/30 g) dried porcini mushrooms

6 tablespoons (3 oz/90 g) unsalted butter

1/2 cup (2 1/2 oz/75 g) finely chopped yellow onion

3/4 lb (375 g) fresh button mushrooms, brushed clean and finely chopped

3/4 lb (375 g) fresh cremini mushrooms, brushed clean and finely chopped

6 tablespoons (2 oz/60 g) all-purpose (plain) flour

1/2 teaspoon salt, plus salt to taste

Ground black pepper to taste

4 cups (32 fl oz/1 l) milk

1 cup (8 fl oz/250 ml) heavy (double) cream

2–3 tablespoons dry sherry

In a small saucepan, combine the broth and porcini and bring to a boil. Cover, remove from the heat, and let stand for 20 minutes. Pour through a fine-mesh sieve lined with dampened cheesecloth (muslin) placed over a small bowl; reserve the liquid. If the porcini feel gritty, rinse with cold water. Squeeze dry and chop finely. Set aside.

In a large saucepan over medium-low heat, melt the butter. Add the onion and sauté for 5 minutes. Increase the heat to medium and add the fresh mushrooms. Cook, stirring, until tender, about 10 minutes. Stir in the reserved chopped porcini. Add the flour, 1/2 teaspoon salt, and a grinding of black pepper, and stir until thoroughly blended. Cook, stirring, for 3 minutes. Gradually add the milk and reserved porcini broth. Cook, stirring, until the mixture boils and thickens, about 10 minutes. Reduce the heat to very low and cook, uncovered, for 10 more minutes; do not boil. Add the cream and cook until very hot but not boiling. Stir in the sherry to taste and season with salt and black pepper.

Ladle into warmed bowls. Serve immediately.

Serves 6

Fish & Shellfish

Salmon Poached in Red Wine

The rich, earthy flavor of salmon makes it one of the few fish fillets to partner perfectly with red wine. Choose a mellow light-bodied varietal to serve at the table. Mashed potatoes with green beans or asparagus are delicious on the side.

Sprinkle the salmon fillets with salt and pepper.

In a sauté pan wide enough to accommodate all the salmon fillets in a single layer, pour in the wine to a depth of 1 1/2–2 inches (4–5 cm). Bring to a boil over high heat. Slip in the salmon fillets, reduce the heat to low so the wine is at a bare simmer, cover, and cook until the salmon is opaque throughout when pierced with a knife, 8–10 minutes. If the fillets are not completely covered by the wine, turn them once at the midpoint so they will take on a uniformly red color. Using a slotted spatula, transfer the salmon to a warmed platter or individual plates and keep warm.

Raise the heat to high, bring the poaching liquid to a boil, and boil until reduced to about 1/2 cup (4 fl oz/125 ml), about 15 minutes, adding the tarragon at the midpoint. The pan juices will be thickened and slightly syrupy. Remove from the heat and swirl in the butter.

Pour the sauce under or over the salmon. Serve at once.

Serves 4

4 salmon fillets, about 6 oz (185 g) each

Salt and ground pepper to taste

2–3 cups (16–24 fl oz/500–750 ml) light red wine

1/4 cup (1/3 oz/10 g) chopped fresh tarragon

1/4 cup (2 oz/60 g) unsalted butter, at room temperature, cut into slivers

Petrale Napoleons with Ratatouille Confit

Petrale sole makes a delicious light alternative to many richer offerings. Here, sole fillets are layered with ratatouille, then more ratatouille is puréed to make a sauce. Sauteed spinach is a fine accompaniment.

1 eggplant (aubergine), ½ lb (250 g), unpeeled, cut into ½-inch (12-mm) dice

1 small yellow onion, chopped

2 teaspoons herbes de Provence

1 yellow bell pepper (capsicum), seeded and cut into ½-inch (12-mm) dice

2 teaspoons sugar

Salt and ground pepper to taste

4 large plum (Roma) tomatoes, seeded and diced

3 large cloves garlic, minced

2 tablespoons tomato paste

3 tablespoons *each* chopped fresh basil and flat-leaf (Italian) parsley

½ cup (4 fl oz/125 ml) chicken broth

4 petrale or lemon sole fillets, about 5 oz (155 g) each

1 teaspoon olive oil

Heat a large nonstick frying pan over medium heat. Coat the pan with nonstick cooking spray. Add the eggplant, onion, and herbes de Provence and sauté until just tender, about 15 minutes. Push the vegetables to one side and coat the pan again with nonstick cooking spray. Add the bell pepper and stir to mix with the vegetables. Season with sugar, salt, and pepper and cook until the bell pepper is tender, about 8 minutes. Stir in the tomatoes and garlic and sauté for 3 minutes. Mix in the tomato paste, cover, and cook until the vegetables are soft, about 5 minutes longer. Remove from the heat and let cool. Stir in 1 tablespoon each of the basil and parsley. Taste and adjust the seasonings.

In a blender, combine ¾ cup (6 oz/185 g) of the eggplant mixture and the broth. Blend until smooth. Transfer the sauce to a saucepan. Set aside the remaining eggplant mixture.

In a small bowl, combine the remaining 2 tablespoons each basil and parsley. Season the sole fillets with salt and pepper. Press the herbs onto 1 side of each fillet. Heat a large nonstick frying pan over medium-high heat. Coat the pan with nonstick cooking spray. Add the fillets, herb sides down, and cook until golden, 2 minutes. Turn and cook until firm, about 1 minute longer. Remove from the heat.

Meanwhile, reheat the sauce and the ratatouille over low heat. Stir the olive oil into the sauce and season with salt and pepper. Separate the fillets in half at their natural seams. Place one-half on each plate, top each equally with the ratatouille, then with the second half of each fillet. Spoon the sauce around the sides. Serve hot.

Serves 4

Salmon with Green Grape Sauce

Verjuice is the fresh juice of underripe or sour grapes. Although it can be found bottled in some well-stocked markets, fresh lime juice makes a worthy substitute

FOR THE SAUCE

1/2 cup (2 oz/60 g) fine dried bread crumbs

1/2 cup (2 1/2 oz/75 g) almonds

2 cloves garlic, chopped

2 tablespoons chopped fresh parsley

1 teaspoon sugar

1/2 teaspoon salt

1/2 teaspoon ground pepper

1 cup (8 fl oz/250 ml) verjuice (see note) or lime juice, strained

1/4 cup (2 fl oz/60 ml) chicken broth

FOR THE SALMON

2 bunches fresh tarragon

1 teaspoon salt

2 lemons, sliced

4 salmon fillets, each about 1/4 lb (125 g) and 1/2 inch (12 mm) thick

To make the sauce, in a blender or food processor, combine the bread crumbs, almonds, garlic, parsley, sugar, salt, and pepper. Purée until nearly smooth. With the motor running, add the grape juice in a slow, steady stream, processing until a smooth paste forms. Set the grape juice mixture aside. Pour the chicken broth into a small saucepan and set aside as well.

To cook the salmon, pour water to a depth of 3 inches (7.5 cm) into a wide, deep sauté pan or saucepan just large enough to hold the salmon fillets in a single layer. Add the tarragon, salt, and lemon slices to the water. Place over high heat, cover, and bring to just below a boil so that the water shimmers with movement but does not bubble. Slip the fillets into the water and poach, uncovered, until the flesh just easily flakes with a fork, about 7 minutes.

Meanwhile, place the saucepan holding the broth over medium heat, bring to a simmer, and stir in the grape juice mixture. Heat, stirring occasionally, until hot. Do not allow to boil or scorch.

Using a spatula, transfer the salmon fillets to 4 individual plates. Spoon 2 or 3 tablespoons of warm sauce over each salmon fillet and serve. Pass the remaining sauce in a warmed bowl at the table.

Serves 4

Halibut with Braised Red Onion

The lemon juice helps the onion keep its color during the slow cooking that softens and sweetens it. Serve with steamed red potatoes and a green salad.

Preheat an oven to 375°F (190°C).

In a large, ovenproof sauté pan over medium-low heat, melt the butter. Add the onions, lemon juice, thyme, salt, and pepper. Toss to coat the onions with the seasonings, then sauté, stirring, until soft, 5–7 minutes. Cover and cook, stirring occasionally and reducing the heat as necessary to keep the onions from browning, until the onions are soft and sweet, 20–25 minutes.

Season the halibut with salt and pepper and place in the pan on top of the onions. Bake, uncovered, until the fish is opaque throughout and just flakes with a fork, about 12 minutes. Check once or twice; if the onions appear to be drying out, add a tablespoon or two of water.

Using a spatula, transfer the fish to warmed dinner plates and drizzle each serving with 1 teaspoon of olive oil. Serve the onions alongside.

Serves 6

3 tablespoons unsalted butter

3 large red (Spanish) onions, halved and thinly sliced

2 tablespoons lemon juice

1 tablespoon minced fresh thyme

Salt and ground pepper to taste

6 skinless halibut fillets, about 6 oz (185 g) each

2 tablespoons olive oil

Saffron Risotto with Scallops

This redolent seafood variation of a classic saffron risotto can be served either as an elegant first course or as a main dish alongside a crisp green salad. Champagne or a light white wine makes a wonderful accompaniment.

6 cups (48 fl oz/1.5 l) fish stock or 3 cups (24 fl oz/750 ml) bottled clam juice mixed with 3 cups (24 fl oz/750 ml) water

6 cups (48 fl oz/1.5 l) water

About 3/4 teaspoon saffron threads

1 1/2 pounds (24 oz/750 g) bay scallops or sea scallops

1/4 cup (2 fl oz/60 ml) olive oil

Salt and freshly ground pepper to taste

4 large shallots, minced

2 cloves garlic, minced

3 cups (21 oz/660 g) Arborio rice

3/4 cup (6 fl oz/180 ml) dry white wine

4 tablespoons unsalted butter, cut into pieces

3 tablespoons minced fresh flat-leaf (Italian) parsley

In a large saucepan over medium heat, combine the fish stock, water, and saffron. Bring just to a simmer, taste, and add more saffron if the saffron flavor is not strong enough. Be careful, however: too much saffron can impart a medicinal taste. Keep the mixture hot but not simmering.

If using sea scallops, cut into $^{1}/_{2}$-inch (12-mm) pieces. In a heavy Dutch oven or soup pot large enough to hold the scallops in a single layer, heat 2 tablespoons of the olive oil over high heat. When the oil is very hot, add the scallops, season with salt and pepper, and sauté just until lightly browned, 1–2 minutes. Transfer to a plate.

Reduce the heat to medium and add the remaining 2 tablespoons olive oil, the shallots, and the garlic. Sauté, stirring, until the shallots are softened, 1–2 minutes. Add the rice and stir until hot throughout, 2–3 minutes. Add the wine and cook, stirring, until it is absorbed, 3–4 minutes. Begin adding the hot broth $^{1}/_{2}$ cup (4 fl oz/125 ml) at a time, stirring often and adding more liquid only when the previous addition has been absorbed. Adjust the heat so that the rice simmers steadily but not briskly. It should take about 25 minutes for the rice to absorb the liquid and become creamy and al dente (tender but firm to the bite). You may not need all the liquid; if you need more, use hot water.

When the rice is almost done, stir in the reserved scallops, butter, and 2 tablespoons of the parsley. Season with salt and pepper. Spoon into warmed shallow serving bowls or plates and garnish with the reserved parsley. Serve at once.

Serves 6

Sautéed Scallops with Orange, Fennel, and Ginger

Scallops offer an inherently succulent, sweet nature well-suited to dining on special occasions. Here, the added nuances of orange, fennel, and ginger contribute a playful platform of tastes that enhances their elegant status. Serve with saffron rice.

Cut off the stems, feathery tops, and any bruised outer stalks from the fennel bulbs. Coarsely chop enough of the feathery tops to yield $^1/_4$ cup ($^1/_3$ oz/10 g) and set aside. Core the fennel bulbs and thinly slice crosswise or lengthwise.

In a sauté pan over medium heat, melt 2 tablespoons of the butter. Add the fennel and sauté, turning often and gradually adding the broth, until the fennel is tender and most of the broth is absorbed, about 10 minutes. Remove from the heat and set aside.

In a large sauté pan over high heat, melt 2 tablespoons of the butter. Add the scallops and sear, turning once, until pale gold on both sides, but still quite soft, 2–3 minutes total. Transfer to a plate.

In the same pan over medium heat, melt 2 tablespoons of the butter. Add the shallots and sauté until softened, about 5 minutes. Add the orange zest, ginger, and wine or vermouth and cook until the liquid is reduced by half, 5–8 minutes. Return the fennel and scallops to the pan and warm through quickly. Stir in the remaining 2 tablespoons butter.

Transfer to a warmed serving dish and sprinkle with the chopped fennel fronds. Serve immediately.

Serves 4

2 fennel bulbs

8 tablespoons (4 oz/125 g) unsalted butter

1 cup (8 fl oz/250 ml) fish or chicken broth

2 lb (1 kg) sea scallops

2 shallots, minced

1 tablespoon grated orange zest

1 teaspoon peeled and grated fresh ginger

1 cup (8 fl oz/250 ml) dry white wine or dry vermouth

Lobster with Cognac Butter

Lobster is a wonderful choice for a New Years' supper or Christmas Eve, but doesn't have to be reserved for special occasions. Here, a simple preparation can make any day feel like a celebration.

4 lobsters, split in half lengthwise and cleaned

2 lemons, cut into wedges

1/4–1/3 cup (2–3 fl oz/60–80 ml) cognac

Leaves from 3 or 4 fresh tarragon sprigs, minced

2 tablespoons unsalted butter, melted, plus 6 tablespoons (3 oz/90 g) unsalted butter

Ground pepper to taste

About 1/3 cup (1/3 oz/10 g) minced mixed fresh herbs such as tarragon, chives, and flat-leaf (Italian) parsley

Preheat an oven to 425°F (220°C). Line 2 rimmed baking sheets with aluminum foil. Arrange the lobster halves crosswise on the sheets, split sides up. Squeeze the juice of 1 lemon over the lobsters and drizzle with about 1 tablespoon cognac. Sprinkle with the minced tarragon leaves, then brush with the melted butter.

Roast the lobsters until the claw and tail meat is opaque, 14–16 minutes. Transfer the lobsters to warmed large individual plates, and tent with aluminum foil to keep warm.

Pour about 1/4 cup (2 fl oz/60 ml) cognac into the pans and stir with a wooden spoon to deglaze them, then pour all the liquid from the pans into a small frying pan. Place the frying pan over high heat. Using a long match, carefully ignite the cognac, then gently tilt the pan back and forth until the flames subside and only a few tablespoons of liquid remain. Working quickly, whisk the 6 tablespoons (3 oz/90 g) butter, 1 tablespoon at a time, into the pan juices until the mixture becomes a creamy sauce. Season with pepper and about 1/4 cup (1/3 oz/10 g) of the minced herbs. Taste and adjust the seasonings.

Spoon the cognac butter into 4 small ramekins and set a ramekin on each plate alongside the lobster. Dividing them evenly, scatter the remaining minced herbs over each serving. Pass the remaining lemon wedges at the table.

Serves 4

Meat & Poultry

Roast Chicken with Rosemary, Garlic, and Lemon

This classic roast chicken preparation is equally at home on the holiday table as it is on the kitchen table when prepared during a busy work week. Rosemary-scented roasted potatoes make a wonderful complement.

1 roasting chicken, 4–4¹⁄₂ lb (2–2.25 kg)

1 lemon, quartered

Kosher salt and ground pepper to taste

8 cloves garlic, crushed

4 fresh rosemary sprigs

¹⁄₃ cup (3 fl oz/80 ml) extra-virgin olive oil

¹⁄₄ cup (2 fl oz/60 ml) lemon juice

1 teaspoon coarsely ground pepper

¹⁄₂ teaspoon table salt

Preheat an oven to 375°F (190°C).

Rinse the chicken and pat dry with paper towels. Rub inside and out with the cut sides of the lemon quarters. Then rub with kosher salt and ground pepper. Place the lemon quarters, 4 of the garlic cloves, and 2 of the rosemary sprigs in the cavity of the chicken. Place, breast side up, on a lightly oiled rack in a roasting pan.

Chop the remaining garlic coarsely. Remove the needles from the remaining rosemary sprigs and chop coarsely.

In a small saucepan over medium heat, combine the chopped garlic and rosemary, the olive oil, lemon juice, coarsely ground pepper, and table salt. Bring to a simmer and simmer until aromatic, about 3 minutes. Remove from the heat.

Roast the chicken, basting with the olive oil mixture every 15 minutes, until an instant-read thermometer inserted into the thickest part of the thigh away from the bone registers 180°F (82°C) or the juices run clear when the thigh joint is pierced, about 1¹⁄₄ hours.

Transfer the chicken to a cutting board and cover loosely with aluminum foil. Let rest for 15 minutes.

Arrange the chicken on a warmed platter. Serve with the skimmed pan juices, if desired.

Serves 4

Pressed Chicken Breasts with Dried Cherries

Pressing the meat during and after roasting intensifies the sweet-tart nature
of the cherry-stuffed chicken breasts. Their pretty red centers are revealed when
the slices are arranged on a platter.

Working with 1 chicken breast half at a time, use a small, sharp knife to cut
a horizontal slit down 1 side and through the center of each breast half, leaving
3 sides uncut. Spoon one-eighth of the dried cherries into each pocket. Firmly press
on each breast with your hand to flatten the meat and seal the edges together.
Arrange in a single layer in a nonaluminum dish.

In a small bowl, stir together the shallots, lemon juice, olive oil, lemon zest,
summer savory, thyme, salt, and pepper. Spoon the shallot mixture evenly over
the chicken breasts. Cover and refrigerate for at least 2 hours or for up to 24 hours.

Preheat a broiler (griller). Transfer the chicken to a broiler pan, reserving the
marinade, and place under the broiler about 4 inches (10 cm) from the heat source.
Broil (grill) until the meat is browned on top, 4–5 minutes.

While the chicken is browning, pour the reserved marinade into a small saucepan
over high heat. Bring to a boil and remove from the heat.

Remove the chicken from the broiler. Set the oven at 375°F (190°C). Transfer the
chicken pieces in a single layer to a shallow baking dish. Pour over the marinade,
and set another baking dish directly on top of the meat. Roast until the juices run
clear when the meat is pierced at the thickest point, 15–20 minutes.

Remove from the oven and set 2 or 3 heavy cans in the top (empty) baking dish
to weight it down. Let rest for at least 20 minutes or for up to 30 minutes. Before
serving, transfer the chicken to a cutting board, and cut crosswise into slices. Spoon
the dish juices over the top. Garnish with parsley.

Serves 6–8

8 skinless, boneless chicken breast halves, 6–7 oz (185–220 g) each

1 cup (4 oz/125 g) pitted dried sweet cherries

2 large shallots, minced

1/4 cup (2 fl oz/60 ml) lemon juice

3 tablespoons olive oil

grated zest of 1/2 lemon

1/2 teaspoon dried summer savory

1/2 teaspoon dried thyme

1/2 teaspoon coarse salt, or to taste

1/2 teaspoon ground pepper, or to taste

Fresh flat-leaf (Italian) parsley sprigs

Coq au Vin

This classic of France's Burgundy region is superb cold-weather fare. Serve it alongside Garlic Mashed Potatoes (page 218) during a cozy holiday weekend with friends. The same wine used for cooking can be delicous as an accompaniment.

2 small chickens, 2–2¹/₂ lb (1–1.25 kg) each, cut into quarters

¹/₂ cup (2¹/₂ oz/75 g) all-purpose (plain) flour

Salt and ground pepper to taste

Ground nutmeg to taste

6 tablespoons (3 oz/90 g) unsalted butter

4 tablespoons (2 fl oz/60 ml) olive oil

3 tablespoons brandy, warmed

2 cups (16 fl oz/500 ml) dry red wine

2 cloves garlic

2 fresh thyme sprigs

1 bay leaf

24 fresh cremini or white button mushrooms, brushed clean and stem ends trimmed

16 pearl onions

2 teaspoons sugar

3–4 tablespoons chopped fresh flat-leaf (Italian) parsley

Rinse the chicken pieces and pat dry with paper towels. Spread the flour on a plate and season with salt, pepper, and nutmeg. Dip the chicken pieces in the seasoned flour, shaking off the excess. Set aside.

In a large frying pan over high heat, warm 2 tablespoons each of the butter and olive oil. Add the chicken in batches and brown on all sides, about 15 minutes. As the pieces are browned, transfer them to a heavy pot. When all the pieces have been browned, pour the brandy over them and ignite with a long match. Let the flame die out, then add the wine, garlic, thyme, and bay leaf. Bring to a boil, cover, reduce the heat to low, and simmer until opaque throughout, about 45 minutes.

Meanwhile, in a sauté pan over high heat, warm 2 tablespoons of the butter and the remaining 2 tablespoons oil. Add the mushrooms and sauté until golden, 6–8 minutes. Transfer to a plate and rinse out the pan.

Bring a saucepan three-fourths full of water to a boil. Add the pearl onions and boil for 2–3 minutes. Drain, cut off the root ends, and slip off the skins. Cut a shallow cross in the root ends. Return the onions to the saucepan, add water just to cover, and bring to a boil. Reduce the heat to low, cover partially, and cook until tender but firm, 10–15 minutes. Drain well. In the rinsed sauté pan over high heat, warm the remaining 2 tablespoons butter. Add the onions and sugar and sauté until lightly caramelized, 4–5 minutes. Remove from the heat.

About 10 minutes before the chicken is done, stir in the mushrooms and onions. Before serving, taste and adjust the seasonings, then sprinkle with parsley.

Serves 4

Chicken Paupiettes with Lemon-Tarragon Sauce

Bring a saucepan three-fourths full of water to a boil. Add the spinach leaves and blanch for 5 seconds. Using a slotted spoon, transfer them to a plate, arranging them so that they may be easily separated; set aside. Add the carrot to the same boiling water and blanch for 2 minutes. Drain and set aside.

Using a meat pounder, pound each chicken breast between 2 sheets of plastic wrap to a thickness of about $1/4$ inch (6 mm). Season the breasts with salt and pepper and place on a work surface. Arrange 3 spinach leaves atop each breast, covering the meat completely. Top the spinach with the prosciutto and then the carrot, again dividing evenly and leaving a $1/2$-inch (12-mm) border on each of the 2 short ends of the chicken. Fold the short sides in over the filling and, beginning from a long side, roll up tightly. Tie each roll at 2-inch (5-cm) intervals with kitchen string.

Heat a nonstick frying pan over medium-high heat. Coat the pan with nonstick cooking spray. Add the rolls, seam sides down, and cook until browned, about 4 minutes. Turn and continue to cook until the chicken is opaque throughout, about 4 minutes longer. Transfer the rolls to a cutting board and let rest for 8–10 minutes.

Meanwhile, in a small saucepan, combine the broth and shallot and bring to a boil over high heat. Boil for about 5 minutes. In a small bowl, stir together the arrowroot and lemon juice until the arrowroot is dissolved, then whisk the mixture into the sauce. Boil until reduced to $1/8$ cup (5 fl oz/160 ml), about 7 minutes.

Remove from the heat and whisk in the fromage blanc and the chopped tarragon. Ladle the sauce onto warmed individual plates. Slice the rolls and fan over the sauce. Garnish with tarragon leaves and serve hot.

Serves 4

12 large spinach leaves

1 carrot, peeled and julienned

4 skinless, boneless chicken breast halves, 5 oz (155 g) each

Salt and ground pepper to taste

2 oz (60 g) thinly sliced prosciutto, trimmed

1 cup (8 fl oz/250 ml) chicken broth

1 large shallot, chopped

2 teaspoons arrowroot

2 tablespoons lemon juice

2 tablespoons fromage blanc

2 teaspoons chopped fresh tarragon, plus leaves for garnish

Herbed Ricotta–Stuffed Chicken Breasts

For a more healthful main course, substitute low-fat ricotta cheese for the whole-milk cheese. Use any leftover stuffing in another recipe, stuffed into slits in thick pork chops, or rolled up in veal scallops. Garnish with sprigs of fresh parsley.

FOR THE STUFFING

2 tablespoons olive oil

2 large shallots, minced

3 large fresh mushrooms, brushed clean and chopped

1 cup (8 oz/250 g) whole-milk ricotta cheese

1/4 cup (1/3 oz/10 g) minced fresh flat-leaf (Italian) parsley

2 tablespoons snipped fresh chives

2 teaspoons chopped fresh tarragon

Coarse salt and ground pepper to taste

2 pinches of freshly grated nutmeg

6 boneless chicken breast halves, 6–7 oz (185–220 g) each, with skin intact

About 1 teaspoon olive oil

Coarse salt and ground pepper to taste

1/2 cup (4 fl oz/125 ml) chicken broth or dry white wine

To make the stuffing, in a small sauté pan over medium heat, warm the olive oil. Add the shallots and sauté until they begin to soften, 1–2 minutes. Add the mushrooms and continue to sauté until tender, about 4 minutes. Let cool.

Meanwhile, in a small bowl, mix the cheese, minced parsley, chives, and tarragon. Stir in the cooled shallot mixture, then season with salt, pepper, and nutmeg.

Preheat an oven to 425°F (220°C). Rinse the chicken breasts and pat dry with paper towels. Carefully slide your fingers under the skin on each breast, separating it from the meat but leaving it attached on one side. Spoon about 1 1/2 tablespoons stuffing onto the meat and pull the skin back in place, covering the filling. Flatten the filling by gently pressing on the skin. Arrange the stuffed breasts in a single layer in a roasting pan. Brush with the olive oil, and season with salt and pepper.

Roast for 15 minutes. Reduce the oven temperature to 375°F (190°C). Continue to roast, basting every 10 minutes with the pan juices, until the skin is crispy brown and the juices run clear when the meat is pierced at the thickest point with a fork, about 30 minutes longer.

Transfer the chicken to a plate and keep warm. Place the roasting pan over high heat. Add the broth or wine, stirring to remove any browned bits from the pan bottom. Bring to a boil and boil until reduced by one-half, about 5 minutes. Spoon off the fat from the pan juices, then strain into a warmed sauceboat.

Arrange each chicken breast on an individual plate. Pass the pan juices at the table.

Serves 6

Sautéed Chicken Breasts with Champagne Grapes

Champagne grapes, also known as Zante, are the tiny grapes that become currants when dried. Look for them in well-stocked markets and farmers' markets during the autumn months. If unavailable, substitute seedless red grapes of any variety.

Rinse the chicken breasts and pat dry with paper towels. In a nonstick frying pan over medium-high heat, melt the butter. When it foams, add the chicken breasts and sear, turning once, until lightly browned, 30–60 seconds on each side. Add 1 tablespoon of the grapes, stir for a few seconds, then add the wine and broth and deglaze the pan, stirring and scraping to dislodge any browned bits from the pan bottom. Reduce the heat to low, cover tightly, and simmer just until the chicken is opaque throughout, 7–8 minutes.

Add the remaining measured grapes and all but 1 teaspoon of the cilantro. Stir well, cover, and cook just long enough to warm the grapes through, 30–60 seconds. Season with the pepper.

Transfer the chicken breasts to warmed individual plates. Pour one-fourth of the pan juices and grapes over each portion. Garnish with the remaining 1 teaspoon cilantro and, if you like, the grape clusters.

Serves 4

4 boneless, skinless chicken breast halves, about 6 oz (185 g) each

2 teaspoons unsalted butter

1 cup (6 oz/185 g) champagne grapes, plus 4 small clusters for garnish (optional)

¼ cup (2 fl oz/60 ml) dry white wine

¼ cup (2 fl oz/60 ml) chicken broth

3 tablespoons minced fresh cilantro (fresh coriander)

¼ teaspoon ground pepper

Risotto with Smoked Chicken and Mushrooms

If your home is full of guests, this recipe can be easily doubled to serve a crowd.
It pairs marvelously with a crisp green salad for a cozy lunch or a light supper.
Use meat cut from smoked chicken breasts or thighs for the best flavor.

5 cups (40 fl oz/1.25 l) chicken broth

2 tablespoons olive oil or unsalted butter

1 shallot, chopped

2 cloves garlic, minced

1 cup (3 oz/90 g) finely chopped fresh portobello, cremini, or porcini mushrooms

1¹/2 cups (10¹/2 oz/330 g) Arborio rice

2 plum (Roma) tomatoes, peeled, seeded, and chopped

2 teaspoons minced fresh thyme

2 teaspoons minced fresh rosemary

2 teaspoons minced fresh marjoram

¹/2 cup (4 fl oz/125 ml) dry white wine

¹/4 lb (125 g) smoked chicken, julienned

Salt and ground pepper to taste

¹/4 cup (¹/2 oz/15 g) chopped fresh flat-leaf (Italian) parsley

Pour the chicken broth into a saucepan and bring to a boil. Reduce the heat to maintain a gentle simmer.

In a large frying pan over medium heat, warm the oil or melt the butter. Add the shallot, garlic, and mushrooms and sauté until softened, about 3 minutes. Stir in the rice and cook, stirring, until the edges are translucent, about 2 minutes. Stir in the tomatoes, thyme, rosemary, and marjoram and sauté for 1 minute longer. Stir in the wine and bring to a boil.

Add a ladleful of the simmering broth and continue to stir constantly over medium heat. When the liquid is almost fully absorbed, add another ladleful. Stir steadily to keep the rice from sticking, and continue to add more liquid, a ladleful at a time, as each previous ladleful is almost absorbed. The risotto is done when the rice is tender but firm, 25–30 minutes. Stir in the chicken and cook briefly to heat through. Season with salt and pepper.

Transfer to a warmed serving dish or individual dishes and sprinkle with the parsley. Serve immediately.

Serves 4

Braised Chicken in White Wine

This dish is inspired by the famed *coq au vin* of the French kitchen, which is traditionally made with red wine. The addition of potatoes makes it a one-pot meal.

4 tablespoons (1¹/₂ oz/45 g) all-purpose (plain) flour

¹/₂ teaspoon salt

¹/₂ teaspoon ground pepper

2 chicken breast halves, about ¹/₂ lb (250 g) each, skinned

2 chicken thighs, about 6 oz (185 g) each, skinned

2 chicken drumsticks, about ¹/₄ lb (125 g) each, skinned

2 tablespoons pure olive oil

3 shallots, chopped

1 carrot, peeled and chopped

1 celery stalk, chopped

¹/₂ lb (250 g) fresh cremini mushrooms, quartered

2 cloves garlic, minced

1 teaspoon minced fresh thyme

2 cups (16 fl oz/500 ml) dry white wine

5 small new potatoes, halved

2 teaspoons unsalted butter

¹/₄ cup (¹/₂ oz/15 g) chopped fresh flat-leaf (Italian) parsley

On a plate, stir together 3 tablespoons of the flour and the salt and pepper. Lightly coat both sides of each chicken piece with the flour mixture, shaking off the excess.

In a wide frying pan over high heat, warm the oil. Add the chicken pieces in batches and sauté, turning once, until browned, about 2 minutes on each side. Transfer to a plate and set aside.

Reduce the heat to medium, add the shallots, carrot, and celery, and sauté until softened, about 4 minutes. Stir in the mushrooms and sauté for 1–2 minutes longer. Then stir in the garlic and sprinkle in the thyme. Raise the heat to high, pour in the wine, and deglaze the pan, stirring to remove any browned bits from the pan bottom.

Return the chicken to the pan and return to a boil. Add the potatoes and reduce the heat to medium-low. Cover and simmer until the chicken is opaque throughout and the juices run clear and the potatoes are tender, about 25 minutes.

Meanwhile, in a small bowl, using your fingers, mix together the butter and the remaining 1 tablespoon flour to form a paste. When the chicken is ready, transfer the pieces to a warmed serving platter. Drop the paste into the sauce bit by bit, stirring to mix. Bring to a boil over high heat and cook, stirring, until the sauce is thickened, about 5 minutes.

Spoon the sauce over the chicken, garnish with the parsley, and serve.

Serves 4

Flemish Chicken with Dried Fruit

The Flanders region of Belgium is home to this delectable stew, originally made with rabbit. Use any of your favorite dried fruits such as apricots, apples, raisins, pitted prunes, or even cherries or cranberries.

In a small bowl, pour the brandy over the fruit and let stand until rehydrated, 15–20 minutes.

Meanwhile, spread the flour on a plate, then lightly coat both sides of each chicken piece with the flour, shaking off the excess.

In a large pot over high heat, warm the oil with the butter. Add the chicken pieces in batches and cook, turning once, until browned, about 2 minutes on each side. Transfer to a plate, season with salt and pepper, and set aside.

Pour off all but 2 tablespoons of the fat from the pot. Place over medium-high heat, add the onion and the leek, if using, and sauté until softened, about 2 minutes. Stir in the garlic and sauté until softened, about 20 seconds. Add the potatoes and thyme. Raise the heat to high, pour in the broth and wine, and deglaze the pot, stirring to remove any browned bits from the bottom. Stir in the rehydrated fruit and brandy, return the chicken to the pot, reduce the heat to medium-low, and simmer, uncovered, until the chicken is opaque throughout and the juices run clear, about 25 minutes.

If the sauce is too thin when the chicken is ready, transfer the chicken pieces to a warmed serving platter and keep warm. Raise the heat to high and boil the sauce until reduced to the desired consistency. Spoon the sauce over the chicken and serve immediately.

Serves 4–6

½ cup (4 fl oz/125 ml) brandy

1 cup (6 oz/185 g) chopped dried fruit (see note)

6 tablespoons (2¼ oz/67 g) all-purpose (plain) flour

2 chicken breast halves, about ½ lb (250 g) each, skinned

4 chicken thighs, about 6 oz (185 g) each, skinned

4 chicken drumsticks, about ¼ lb (125 g) each, skinned

1 lb (500 g) chicken wings

2 tablespoons canola oil

1 tablespoon unsalted butter

Salt and ground pepper to taste

1 yellow onion, chopped

1 leek, white part only, chopped (optional)

3 cloves garlic, minced

2 or 3 new potatoes, cubed

1 teaspoon dried thyme

2 cups (16 fl oz/500 ml) chicken broth

1 cup (8 fl oz/250 ml) white wine

Chicken Sauté with Madeira Sauce

The rich depth of sweet-tart Madeira marries perfectly with the light flavors of sautéed chicken breasts. The sauce gives the easy-to-prepare dish an elegance, making it a good candidate for a special dinner when you are pressed for time.

One at a time, place the chicken breasts between 2 sheets of plastic wrap and flatten with a meat pounder until an even $1/2$ inch (12 mm) thick. Spread the flour on a plate, then lightly coat both sides of each breast with the flour, shaking off the excess.

In a frying pan over high heat, melt the butter with the oil. Add the chicken breasts and sauté, turning once, until just beginning to brown, 1–2 minutes on each side. Transfer to a platter, season with salt and pepper, and set aside.

Pour off any fat from the pan and return to high heat. Pour in the broth and deglaze the pan, stirring to remove any browned bits from the pan bottom. Bring to a boil, add the dry and sweet wines, and boil until reduced by half, about 5 minutes. Return the chicken to the pan and reduce the heat to medium. Cook, turning once or twice, until the chicken is opaque throughout and the juices run clear, about 5 minutes longer. Transfer the chicken to a warmed platter; keep warm.

Stir the cream to taste into the pan juices and cook over medium-high heat just until slightly thickened, about 2 minutes. Pour over the chicken. Garnish with the parsley and serve.

Serves 4

4 skinless, boneless chicken breast halves, about 6 oz (185 g) each

2 tablespoons all-purpose (plain) flour

1 tablespoon unsalted butter

1 tablespoon canola or safflower oil

salt and ground white or black pepper to taste

1 cup (8 fl oz/250 ml) chicken broth

$1/2$ cup (4 fl oz/125 ml) Sauvignon Blanc or other dry wine

$1/3$ cup (3 fl oz/80 ml) Madeira or other sweet wine

2–4 tablespoons heavy (double) cream

$1/4$ cup ($1/2$ oz/15 g) chopped fresh flat-leaf (Italian) parsley

Chicken in Green Mole

5 chicken breast halves, 1/2 lb (250 g) each

12 chicken thighs, 1/2 lb (250 g) each

1 yellow onion, halved

1 piece peeled fresh ginger, about 1 inch (2.5 cm)

2 1/2 teaspoons salt, plus salt to taste

1 teaspoon peppercorns

4 Anaheim or poblano chiles

2 serrano chiles

5 tomatillos, husks removed

2 tablespoons vegetable oil

1 tablespoon shelled pumpkin seeds

10 blanched almonds

2 teaspoons sesame seeds

1/2 yellow onion, chopped

1 green bell pepper (capsicum), quartered and seeded

1 tomato, seeded and chopped

2 cloves garlic, chopped

1 tablespoon peanut butter

2 whole allspice berries

1 large head romaine (cos) lettuce, coarsely chopped

1 cup (1 oz/30 g) fresh parsley leaves

1 corn tortilla, if needed

Put all the chicken pieces in a large, heavy saucepan. Add water just to cover and the onion, ginger, 1 teaspoon of the salt, and peppercorns. Bring to a boil, skimming any foam that rises to the surface. Reduce the heat to low, cover, and simmer until the chicken is tender and the juices run clear when a thigh is pierced, about 40 minutes. Transfer the chicken pieces to a baking dish and cover to keep warm. Using a large spoon, skim off the fat from the stock; reserve the stock.

Meanwhile, preheat a broiler (griller). Place the chiles and tomatillos on a broiler pan and slip under the broiler. Broil (grill), turning as needed, just until the skins are evenly blackened and blistered. Place on a plate, cover with aluminum foil, and let stand 10 minutes. Peel away the skins from the chiles, then cut in half lengthwise, remove the seeds, and coarsely chop the chiles. Cut the tomatillos into quarters. In a blender or food processor, combine the chiles and tomatillos with 1 cup (8 fl oz/ 250 ml) of the reserved stock. Purée until smooth.

In a sauté pan over medium heat, warm the vegetable oil. Add the pumpkin seeds and almonds and sauté until lightly golden, 3–4 minutes. Add the sesame seeds and sauté for 2 minutes longer. Transfer to the chile mixture along with the onion, bell pepper, tomato, garlic, peanut butter, allspice, remaining 1 1/2 teaspoons salt, and 1/2 cup (4 fl oz/125 ml) of the reserved stock. Purée until smooth. Add the lettuce and parsley and process again. The mixture should be thick, not watery. If it is too thick, thin with a little more stock; if too thin, tear the tortilla into pieces, add some to the stock, and process until thickened. Taste and add salt if needed.

Transfer the sauce to a saucepan and place over low heat. Cook until the color changes from a bright to a darker green, 10–15 minutes. Remove the skin from the chicken and transfer to a serving platter. Pour the hot sauce over the chicken and serve at once.

Serves 10

Chicken Sauté with Artichokes

Fresh artichokes taste best in this dish. If unavailable, use about 1¹/₂ cups (12 oz/375 g) thawed, frozen hearts or drained, marinated hearts and add them with the tomatoes. Sprinkle with chopped fresh flat-leaf (Italian) parsley just before serving.

Have ready a bowl three-fourths full of water to which you have added the juice from ¹/₂ lemon. Working with 1 artichoke at a time, cut off the stem even with the base. Cut off the top third of the artichoke. Remove 3 or 4 rows of the tough outer leaves. Peel away any dark green areas around the base. Rub the cut surfaces with the remaining lemon half to prevent darkening. Cut in half lengthwise and, using a sharp spoon or knife, scoop out and discard the prickly choke. Then cut each half in half again to create quarters and add to the lemon water. Set aside.

Spread the flour on a plate, then lightly coat both sides of each chicken piece with the flour, shaking off the excess. In a frying pan over high heat, warm the oil. Add the chicken pieces and sauté, turning once, until lightly browned, 1–2 minutes on each side. Transfer to a platter, season with salt and pepper, and set aside.

Pour off all but 2 tablespoons of the fat from the pan. Reduce the heat to medium, add the garlic and shallot, and sauté until softened, 1–2 minutes. Stir in the herbs and mustard. Raise the heat to high, pour in the wine and broth, and deglaze the pan, stirring to remove any browned bits from the pan bottom. Return the chicken to the pan and add the tomatoes. Reduce the heat to medium-high and cook, turning the chicken occasionally, until the chicken is opaque throughout, about 20 minutes for the breasts and 30 minutes for the thighs and drumsticks. About 10 minutes before the chicken is done, drain the artichokes and add to the pan. Transfer the chicken pieces to a plate as they are done, then just before the remaining chicken is done, return the cooked pieces to the pan to warm briefly. Transfer to a warmed serving platter and serve at once.

Serves 4–6

1 lemon, halved

1 lb (500 g) small artichokes

3 tablespoons all-purpose (plain) flour

2 chicken breast halves, about ¹/₂ lb (250 g) each, skinned

2 chicken thighs, about 6 oz (185 g) each, skinned

2 chicken drumsticks, about ¹/₄ lb (125 g) each, skinned

2 tablespoons pure olive oil

Salt and ground pepper to taste

4 cloves garlic, cut into slivers

1 shallot, cut into slivers

1 tablespoon *each* minced fresh basil, tarragon, and chervil

1 tablespoon Dijon mustard

1 cup (8 fl oz/250 ml) dry white wine

¹/₂ cup (4 fl oz/125 ml) chicken broth

2 or 3 plum (Roma) tomatoes, seeded and chopped

Chicken and Dumplings

Here is a traditional American Sunday dinner that couldn't be easier to prepare. A potful of chicken and vegetables topped with plump dumplings is comfort food at its best.

1 chicken, 3½–4 lb (1.75–2 kg)

2 celery stalks, chopped

2 carrots, peeled and sliced

1 green bell pepper (capsicum), seeded and chopped

1 rutabaga, peeled and cubed

1 parsnip, peeled and cubed

1 yellow onion, chopped

3 cloves garlic, minced

1 bay leaf

2 teaspoons salt

1 teaspoon dried thyme

½ teaspoon ground pepper

FOR THE DUMPLINGS

1 cup (5 oz/155 g) all-purpose (plain) flour

1½ teaspoons baking powder

½ teaspoon salt

3 tablespoons unsalted butter

¼ cup (⅓ oz/10 g) finely chopped flat-leaf (Italian) parsley

¼ cup (2 fl oz/60 ml) milk

Place the whole chicken, breast side up, in a dutch oven or other large pot. Add the celery, carrots, bell pepper, rutabaga, parsnip, onion, garlic, bay leaf, salt, thyme, and pepper, distributing the vegetables and seasonings evenly around and over the chicken. Add water just to cover. Bring to a boil over high heat. Reduce the heat to medium-low, cover, and simmer until the chicken is opaque throughout and the juices run clear and the vegetables are tender, about 50 minutes.

While the chicken is cooking, make the dumpling dough: In a bowl, stir together the flour, baking powder, and salt. Add the butter and, using a pastry blender or your fingers, work in the butter until the mixture resembles coarse crumbs. Add the parsley. Using a fork, stir in the milk until a firm dough forms. Pinch off pieces of dough and roll into balls. You should have enough dough for 8–10 dumplings.

When the chicken is ready, using tongs, transfer it to a cutting board or platter and cover loosely with aluminum foil to keep warm.

Raise the heat under the pot to medium-high. Bring the broth to a boil, skimming off any foam that rises to the surface. Using a slotted spoon, lower the dumplings into the boiling broth. Cover and cook until the dumplings puff and the interiors are uniformly set, 10–15 minutes. To test, cut into the center of a dumpling.

Carve the chicken into serving pieces or bite-sized pieces and transfer to individual bowls. Using a slotted spoon, place 1 or 2 dumplings in each bowl. Ladle the broth into the bowls and serve.

Serves 4–6

Braised Chicken Provençale

Chicken thighs are better suited for braising than lean chicken breasts. They don't dry out as quickly, and their fuller flavor can stand up to this zesty sauce.

In a large sauté pan, warm the olive oil over medium-high heat until hot. Working in batches, add the chicken thighs, skin side down, without crowding. Season with salt and pepper. Reduce the heat to medium and cook until browned on the bottoms, about 6 minutes. Turn, season with salt and pepper, and cook until browned on the bottoms, about 2 minutes. Transfer to a large plate.

Remove the pan from the heat and discard all but 2 tablespoons of the fat from the pan. Add the garlic to the pan and cook, stirring, for 1 minute. Add the tomatoes, anchovies, wine, and thyme. Stir to blend, then return the chicken to the frying pan, skin side up. Cover, adjust the heat to maintain a gentle simmer, and cook until the chicken is no longer pink at the bone, about 20 minutes.

Using a slotted spoon, transfer the chicken to a warmed serving platter. Add the olives to the frying pan and cook until heated through. If the sauce is a little thin, continue to cook over medium-high heat until reduced to the desired consistency. Taste, adding salt and pepper as needed. Pour the sauce over the chicken and serve at once.

Serves 6

2 tablespoons olive oil

12 small chicken thighs (about 3 lb/1.5 kg total), rinsed and patted dry

Salt and ground pepper, to taste

4 to 6 garlic cloves, minced

1 can (28 oz/875 g) crushed tomatoes with their juices

6 anchovy fillets in olive oil (about one 2 oz/60 g tin), drained and minced

1/3 cup (3 fl oz/80 ml) dry white wine

2 1/2 teaspoons minced fresh thyme

1/2 cup (4 oz/125 g) Niçoise or kalamata olives, pitted and coarsely chopped

Classic Barbeque Chicken

Ancho chiles—dried poblano peppers—have a sweet, earthy flavor with just a touch of heat. For a barbecued bird with more bite, add ½ teaspoon or more cayenne pepper to the marinade and marinate the chicken overnight.

1 ancho chile, seeded and cut into pieces

1 cup (8 fl oz/250 ml) boiling water

1 tablespoon olive oil

2 chickens, about 3½ lb (1.75 kg) each, cut into serving pieces

BARBECUE SAUCE

2 tablespoons unsalted butter

1 yellow onion, finely chopped

1½ cups (12 fl oz/375 ml) ketchup

½ cup (4 fl oz/125 ml) water

⅓ cup (3 fl oz/80 ml) Worcestershire sauce

¼ cup (2 fl oz/60 ml) steak sauce

2 tablespoons cider vinegar

⅓ cup (2½ oz/75 g) firmly packed brown sugar

In a small heatproof bowl, combine the ancho chile and boiling water. Let stand until the chile has softened, about 20 minutes. Drain, reserving ¼ cup (2 fl oz/60 ml) of the liquid. In a food processor or blender, combine the softened ancho, reserved liquid, and olive oil. Process until smooth. Rub the chicken with the paste and place in a shallow nonaluminum dish. Cover and refrigerate for at least 2 hours or for up to 24 hours. Remove from the refrigerator 30 minutes before grilling.

Meanwhile, make the sauce: In a saucepan over medium-low heat, melt the butter. Add the onion and cook for 5 minutes. Stir in the ketchup, water, Worcestershire sauce, steak sauce, vinegar, and brown sugar. Bring to a boil, reduce the heat to low, cover partially, and simmer until thickened slightly, about 20 minutes. Set aside.

Prepare a hot fire in a covered grill. Position the grill rack 4–6 inches (10–15 cm) above the fire. Place the drumsticks and thighs on the center of the rack. Cover the grill and open the vents halfway. Cook, turning once, until browned, about 7 minutes on each side. Move to the outer edges of the rack and place the breasts and wings in the center. Cover and cook, turning once, until browned and the juices run clear when a thigh is pierced, about 8 minutes on each side. Meanwhile, reheat the barbecue sauce. Transfer ½ cup (4 fl oz/120 ml) of the sauce to a small bowl. Brush the chicken with ¼ cup (2 fl oz/60 ml) of the reserved barbecue sauce. Turn over the chicken and brush with the remaining ¼ cup (2 fl oz/ 60 ml) sauce. Continue to cook uncovered, turning once, until crisp, about 2 minutes on each side. Transfer to a platter and serve. Pass the remaining sauce at the table.

Serves 6

Roasted Turkey with Barley Stuffing

To make the stuffing, in a wide saucepan, combine the water, orange slice, cinnamon stick, celery top, carrot, and salt. Stick the whole cloves into the onion half, add to the pan, and bring to a boil. Stir in the barley, cover, reduce the heat to low, and cook until the barley is plump and tender, about 55 minutes. Drain off any water left in the pan. Discard the vegetables and spices. Set the barley aside.

In a large frying pan over medium heat, melt the butter. Add the chopped onion and cook, stirring often, for 10 minutes. Stir in the apricots, prunes, raisins, and almonds. Stir in the barley and cook for 10 minutes. Stir in the lemon juice. Set aside.

Preheat an oven to 325°F (165°C). Rinse the turkey and pat dry with paper towels. Place the turkey, breast side up, on a rack in a roasting pan. Squeeze the lemon juice inside and outside the turkey, then rub the skin with the lemon halves. Sprinkle with salt and pepper. Spoon some stuffing into the neck cavity; pull the skin over the stuffing and secure with small skewers. Spoon the remaining stuffing into the larger cavity, packing it loosely. Place any leftover stuffing in a baking dish, cover tightly, and set aside. Cross the drumsticks and, using kitchen string, tie the legs together. Tuck the wings underneath the body. Spread the surface of the turkey with 2 tablespoons of the butter; melt the remaining 2 tablespoons and set aside. Cover the pan with heavy-duty aluminum foil or with its lid.

Roast, basting every 20 minutes with the pan juices and the melted butter, for 2¹⁄₂ hours. Uncover and continue to roast, basting often, until well browned, the juices run clear when a thigh is pierced with a knife, and an instant-read thermometer inserted into the thickest part of a thigh registers 170°F (77°C), 1–1¹⁄₂ hours longer.

Remove from the oven and let stand for 30 minutes. Meanwhile, bake the leftover stuffing for 30 minutes. Remove the skewers and string, spoon the stuffing into a bowl, carve the turkey, and arrange on a platter. Pass the stuffing at the table.

Serves 10–12

FOR THE STUFFING

8 cups (64 fl oz/2 l) water

1 thick orange slice

1 cinnamon stick

1 leafy celery stalk top

1 carrot, halved

1 tablespoon salt

2 whole cloves

¹⁄₂ yellow onion, plus 2 cups (8 oz/250 g) chopped yellow onion

2 cups (1 lb/500 g) pearl barley

¹⁄₂ cup (4 oz/125 g) unsalted butter

1 cup (6 oz/185 g) *each* dried apricot halves and pitted prunes, quartered

¹⁄₂ cup (3 oz/90 g) dark or golden raisins (sultanas)

1 cup (5 oz/155 g) coarsely chopped almonds

¹⁄₄ cup (2 fl oz/60 ml) lemon juice

1 turkey, 12–14 lb (6–7 kg), giblets and neck removed

1 lemon, halved

Salt and ground pepper to taste

4 tablespoons (2 oz/60 g) unsalted butter

Glazed Turkey Breast with Corn Bread Stuffing

1 cup (5 oz/155 g) *each* all-purpose (plain) flour and yellow cornmeal

1 tablespoon *each* sugar and baking powder

1¹/₂ teaspoons salt

¹/₄ teaspoon ground pepper, plus pepper to taste

1 cup (8 fl oz/250 ml) milk

¹/₄ cup (2 oz/60 g) unsalted butter, melted, plus ¹/₄ cup (2 oz/60 g) unsalted butter

1 egg, lightly beaten

2 cups (8 oz/250 g) chopped sweet onion such as Vidalia

1¹/₂ cups (6 oz/185 g) peeled, cored, and chopped apple

1 cup (4¹/₂ oz/140 g) *each* chopped celery and chopped pecans

1 cinnamon stick

1 bone-in turkey breast, 6–7 lb (3–3.5 kg), rinsed and dried

4 tablespoons lemon juice

Salt and ground pepper to taste

2 tablespoons unsalted butter

¹/₃ cup (4 oz/125 g) honey

1 teaspoon ground cinnamon

¹/₄ teaspoon ground allspice

To make the corn bread, preheat an oven to 400°F (200°C). Lightly butter a 9-inch (23-cm) square baking pan. In a bowl, mix the flour, cornmeal, sugar, baking powder, ¹/₂ teaspoon of the salt, and the ¹/₄ teaspoon pepper. Stir in the milk, melted butter, and egg. Spread the batter into the prepared pan. Bake until the top is firm, about 20 minutes. Let cool, then crumble coarsely into a bowl.

To make the stuffing, in a large frying pan over medium heat, melt the ¹/₄ cup (2 oz/60 g) butter. Add the onion, apple, and celery. Sauté until softened, about 5 minutes. Add the pecans and sauté for 5 minutes. Add the corn bread crumbs, cinnamon stick, the remaining 1 teaspoon salt, and pepper to taste. Let cool.

Preheat the oven to 350°F (180°C). Place the turkey breast, skin side up, in an aluminum foil–lined roasting pan. Sprinkle with 2 tablespoons of the lemon juice, and the salt and pepper. Using your fingers, make a pocket on either side of the breastbone between the skin and the meat and spread the butter inside. Spoon about 1 cup (8 oz/250 g) stuffing into the neck opening. Secure the skin over the opening with a skewer. Spoon the remaining stuffing into the large cavity, using the foil liner to hold it in place. Cover the breast loosely with more foil. Roast for 45 minutes. Meanwhile, make a glaze: In a small saucepan over low heat, combine the honey, remaining 2 tablespoons lemon juice, cinnamon, and allspice. Bring to a boil, stirring, then remove from the heat.

Remove the breast from the oven, uncover, and coat with half of the glaze. Continue to roast uncovered, brushing with the remaining glaze every 15 minutes, for about 1 hour. It is done when an instant-read thermometer inserted into the meat registers 160°F (71°C), or the juices run clear when it is pierced with a knife. Remove from the oven. Let stand for 10 minutes in the pan. Spoon the stuffing into a bowl. Thinly slice the breast and arrange on a warmed platter. Pass the stuffing.

Serves 10–12

Curried Cornish Hens

This dish is sublimely delicious served atop spiced couscous. Try adding sautéed onion and ginger, cooked diced carrots, cooked English peas, currants, minced garlic, and sliced (flaked) almonds to regular cooked couscous for an especially flavorful variation.

To make the curried Cornish hens, in a small, dry frying pan over low heat, toast the curry powder, shaking the pan, just until it begins to warm and give off its aroma, about 20 seconds. Remove from the heat and transfer to a small bowl. Add the butter, orange zest, and salt and pepper. Using a fork, mash the spices into the butter until well blended. Cover and refrigerate until the butter is hard, about 30 minutes.

Meanwhile, preheat an oven to 350°F (180°C). Rinse the hens and pat dry. Sprinkle inside and outside with salt and pepper. Stick each onion wedge with a whole clove. Place 1 onion wedge, 1 ginger slice, 1 orange zest strip, 1 garlic clove, and 1 bay leaf in the cavity of each hen. Cross the drumsticks on each bird and, using kitchen string, tie together. Starting at the neck opening, loosen the breast skin from the meat to make a small pocket. Cut the curried butter into 8 pieces and slip 1 piece under the skin of each hen, positioning it in the center of each breast. Arrange the hens, breast sides up, in a large baking pan.

Roast, basting with the pan juices every 20 minutes, until the hens are golden brown and the juices run clear when a thigh is pierced with a knife, about 1 hour.

Remove the strings from the hens and serve at once.

Serves 8

4 teaspoons Madras curry powder

1/2 cup (4 oz/125 g) unsalted butter, at room temperature

1 teaspoon grated orange zest

Salt and ground pepper to taste

8 Cornish hens, 1 lb (500 g) each

8 *each:* yellow onion wedges; whole cloves; peeled fresh ginger slices; orange zest strips (about 2 inches/5 cm long); garlic cloves, lightly crushed; and bay leaves

Roast Duck with Cranberry Glaze & Relish

2 ducks, 4¹/₂–5¹/₂ lb (2.25–2.75 kg) each, thawed in the refrigerator if frozen

2 tablespoons lemon juice

Salt and ground pepper to taste

1 yellow onion, quartered

4 whole cloves

1 orange, quartered

2 bay leaves

FOR THE GLAZE

1 can (1 lb/500 g) jellied cranberry sauce

2 tablespoons lemon juice

1 teaspoon grated lemon zest

¹/₂ teaspoon salt

¹/₄ teaspoon ground cloves

FOR THE CRANBERRY RELISH

1 cup (8 oz/250 g) sugar

¹/₂ cup (4 fl oz/125 ml) water

3 cups (12 oz/375 g) fresh or frozen cranberries

¹/₂ cup (3 oz/90 g) golden raisins (sultanas)

2 teaspoons grated lemon zest

1 tablespoon aged red wine vinegar

Ground pepper to taste

Rinse the ducks and pat dry. Sprinkle inside and out with the lemon juice, salt, and pepper. Pierce each onion quarter with 1 whole clove. Stuff each duck cavity with 2 onion quarters, 2 orange quarters, and 1 bay leaf. Cross the drumsticks and, using kitchen string, tie the legs together. Using a knife tip, pierce the skin of each duck at 1-inch (2.5-cm) intervals to allow the fat to cook out from under the skin.

Preheat an oven to 350°F (180°C).

To make the glaze, in a saucepan over medium heat, combine the cranberry sauce, lemon juice, lemon zest, salt, and ground cloves. Heat, stirring, until melted, about 5 minutes. Lightly brush the entire surface of the ducks with some of the glaze. Arrange the ducks, breast sides up, on a rack in a large roasting pan.

Roast, basting every 30 minutes with the cranberry glaze. As excess fat accumulates in the roasting pan, use a bulb baster to remove it. After the first hour of roasting, carefully turn over the ducks onto their breasts and roast, breasts down, for 1 hour. Then turn the ducks breasts up again and continue to roast until the breast skin is golden and crisp and the meat at the leg joint is cooked through when cut into, about 30 minutes longer. The ducks should cook in about 2¹/₂ hours total.

While the ducks are roasting, make the cranberry relish: In a large sauté pan, combine the sugar and water over medium-low heat. Cook, stirring, until the mixture turns a golden amber, 5–10 minutes. Add the cranberries, raisins, and lemon zest all at once. Cook, stirring to break up any sugar lumps, until the cranberries pop and the mixture is thick, about 10 minutes. Remove from the heat. Stir in the vinegar and pepper. Transfer to a bowl and set aside.

When the ducks are ready, transfer them to a cutting board and let stand for 10 minutes. Cut into quarters and set on a warmed platter. Pass the relish at the table.

Serves 8–10

Braised Duck Thighs with Fresh Plums

Prune plums—also known as Italian, French, or sugar plums—are a seasonal specialty of late summer and early autumn. If unavailable, substitute with any fresh plum variety. Serve with spaetzle and garlic-sautéed chard, if you like.

Sprinkle the salt in a nonstick frying pan just large enough to hold the 4 duck thighs. Place the pan over high heat. When the pan is hot, place the thighs in it and sprinkle them with the pepper. Sear, turning once, until browned, 1–2 minutes on each side. Pour in the brandy and add half of the plums. Reduce the heat to medium-high and deglaze the pan, stirring to dislodge any browned bits from the pan bottom, 1–2 minutes.

In a small bowl, dissolve the sugar in 4 tablespoons (2 fl oz/60 ml) chicken broth and pour into the pan. Reduce the heat to low and cover tightly. Cook for 7–8 minutes. Uncover and check to see if the pan has dried out. If it has, add another 1 tablespoon broth. Turn over the duck, cover the pan, and continue to cook until the duck is cooked through and tender, 7–8 minutes longer. Transfer the duck pieces to a plate.

Skim or pour off any fat from the pan. There should be about 2 tablespoons of juices remaining in the pan. Return the pan to medium-low heat and return the thighs and any collected juices on the plate to the pan along with the remaining plums. Cook, turning the thighs once, until the just-added plums are heated through, 2–3 minutes.

To serve, transfer the duck thighs to warmed individual plates and spoon some of the sauce and plums over them. Serve immediately.

Serves 4

1 teaspoon salt

4 skinless duck thighs

1 teaspoon ground pepper

¼ cup (2 fl oz/60 ml) brandy

8 prune plums, halved and pitted

1 teaspoon sugar

4–5 tablespoons (2–2½ fl oz/60–75 ml) chicken broth

Duck Breasts with Black Cherry Sauce

Available at many high-quality butcher shops, boneless duck breasts are ideally suited for grilling—the perfect way to eliminate some of their fat. Serve the duck rosy pink, drizzled with the savory cherry sauce.

2 boneless whole duck breasts, about 1³/₄ lb (875 g) each

¹/₄ cup (2 fl oz/60 ml) olive oil

¹/₄ cup (2 fl oz/60 ml) orange juice

¹/₂ teaspoon peeled and minced fresh ginger

¹/₂ teaspoon salt

¹/₄ teaspoon red pepper flakes

BLACK CHERRY SAUCE

1 jar (12 oz/375 g) black cherry preserves

¹/₂ cup (4 fl oz/125 ml) bottled chili sauce

¹/₂ cup (4 fl oz/125 ml) beef broth

1 tablespoon hoisin sauce

¹/₂ teaspoon Dijon mustard

1 tablespoon snipped fresh chives

Cut each duck breast in half. Using a sharp knife, cut several long slashes in the skin, taking care not to cut through to the meat. Place the breasts in a shallow nonaluminum dish just large enough to hold them in a single layer.

In a small bowl, mix the olive oil, orange juice, ginger, salt, and pepper flakes. Pour over the duck breasts, and turn to coat. Cover and refrigerate, turning the breasts often, for 2 hours. Remove from the refrigerator 30 minutes before grilling.

Meanwhile, make the sauce: In a saucepan over medium-low heat, combine the cherry preserves, chili sauce, beef broth, hoisin sauce, and mustard. Stir well and bring to a boil. Reduce the heat to low, cover partially, and simmer until thickened, about 20 minutes. Remove from the heat.

Prepare a hot fire in a grill. Position the grill rack 4–6 inches (10–15 cm) above the fire. Place the duck breasts, skin sides down, on the rack. Cook until the skin is crisp, about 5 minutes. Turn over the breasts and continue to cook until medium-rare, about 3 minutes longer. Brush both sides of the breasts with a little of the black cherry sauce and grill for 1 minute on each side to glaze. Transfer the breasts to a cutting board, cover loosely with aluminum foil, and let stand for 5 minutes. Meanwhile, reheat the cherry sauce over low heat.

Carve the duck breasts on the diagonal across the grain into thin slices. Arrange on a warmed platter and spoon the hot cherry sauce over the top. Sprinkle with the chives and serve at once.

Serves 4

Orange-Ginger Pork Tenderloins

The redolent flavors of orange and ginger offer just the right amount of flattery to tender slices of grilled pork. A side of crisp sesame-scented coleslaw and thick wedges of fresh-cut orange add subtle oriental flair.

2 pork tenderloins, about 1 lb (500 g) each, trimmed of fat

1/2 cup (4 fl oz/125 ml) thawed frozen orange juice concentrate

4 teaspoons soy sauce

1 tablespoon dry sherry

1 teaspoon Asian sesame oil

2 teaspoons peeled and grated fresh ginger

1 teaspoon minced garlic

1 teaspoon dried thyme

FOR THE GLAZE

1/4 cup (2 fl oz/60 ml) thawed frozen orange juice concentrate

2 tablespoons molasses

2 teaspoons peeled and grated fresh ginger

1/4 teaspoon dried thyme

1/4 teaspoon ground pepper

Salt to taste

1 orange, cut into 6 wedges

Fresh thyme sprigs (optional)

Pat the tenderloins dry. Place in a shallow nonaluminum dish or lock-top plastic bag. In a small bowl, stir together the 1/2 cup (4 fl oz/125 ml) orange juice concentrate, soy sauce, sherry, sesame oil, ginger, garlic, and thyme. Pour over the pork and cover the dish or seal the bag. Refrigerate for at least 6 hours or for as long as overnight, turning the meat occasionally. Bring to room temperature before cooking.

Prepare a medium-hot fire in a grill. Position the grill rack 4–5 inches (10–13 cm) above the fire.

To make the glaze, in small bowl, stir together the 1/4 cup (2 fl oz/60 ml) orange juice concentrate, molasses, ginger, thyme, and pepper. Set aside.

Remove the tenderloins from the marinade and grill, turning frequently, for 15 minutes. Brush generously with some of the glaze and continue grilling, basting frequently, until an instant-read thermometer inserted into the thickest part of the meat registers 150°F (65°C), about 15 minutes longer. (The meat should have a rosy hue at the center when cut into with a sharp knife.)

Transfer to a cutting board, cover loosely with aluminum foil, and let rest for 10 minutes. To serve, cut the tenderloins crosswise on a sharp diagonal into slices 1/4 inch (6 mm) thick. Arrange the slices, overlapping them, on a serving plate, season lightly with salt, and brush with any remaining glaze. Garnish with the orange wedges and thyme sprigs, if using.

Serves 6

Braised Pork Chop with Cabbage

In a large ovenproof sauté pan or Dutch oven over medium heat, warm the olive oil. Season the pork chops on both sides with salt, pepper, and paprika. When the oil is hot, add the pork chops, in batches if necessary to avoid crowding, and brown, turning once, 1–2 minutes on each side. Transfer to a platter.

Pour off any oil in the pan, let the pan cool for a minute, and then add the butter. Return the pan to medium-low heat. When the butter melts, add the onions. Sauté, stirring, until softened, 5–7 minutes. Do not let the onions brown. Add the cabbage and caraway seeds, season with salt and pepper, and stir to mix with the onions. Cover and cook until the cabbage is almost tender, 12–15 minutes, reducing the heat if necessary so the vegetables cook without browning.

Place the pork chops on top of the cabbage, cover, and cook over medium-low heat until the pork chops are no longer pink when cut into at the center but still juicy, about 10 minutes. Do not overcook.

Transfer the cabbage and pork chops to warmed dinner plates. Serve hot.

Serves 6

2 tablespoons olive oil

6 pork loin chops, about 8 oz (250 g) each

Salt, ground pepper, and paprika to taste

6 tablespoons unsalted butter, cut into pieces

2 large yellow onions, thinly sliced

1 medium head green cabbage, cored and thinly sliced

3/4 teaspoon caraway seeds

Apple-Stuffed Pork Loin

To make the stuffing, in a large frying pan over medium-low heat, warm the olive oil. Add the apple and onion and sauté until golden, about 5 minutes. Stir in the garlic and cook for 1 minute. Add the dried apples, raisins, and thyme and season with salt and pepper. Add the apple cider and boil, stirring occasionally, until the cider is absorbed by the stuffing, about 5 minutes. Let cool slightly.

Preheat an oven to 400°F (200°C). Have ready 4 pieces of kitchen string, each 18 inches (45 cm) long. Butterfly the pork loin by making a slit down its length, cutting just deep enough so that it lays flat. Do not cut all the way through. Spoon the stuffing evenly onto the meat. Close up the loin and, using the strings, tie at even intervals so it assumes its original shape. Sprinkle with the $1/4$ teaspoon thyme and season with salt and pepper.

Place in a baking pan and add $1/2$ cup (4 fl oz/125 ml) of the cider to the pan. Roast the loin for 30 minutes. Baste with the pan juices and add the remaining $1/2$ cup (4 fl oz/125 ml) cider to the pan. Continue to roast, basting occasionally with the pan juices, until the meat is pale pink when cut, or until an instant-read thermometer inserted into the thickest point registers 160°F (71°C), about 45 minutes longer.

Transfer the loin to a cutting board and cover with a piece of aluminum foil. Scrape the pan bottom to dislodge any remaining bits, then pour the pan juices into a measuring pitcher and add more cider as needed to measure $1 1/2$ cups (12 fl oz/375 ml) total. In a small saucepan, combine $1/4$ cup (2 fl oz/60 ml) of the pan juices and the cornstarch; stir until the cornstarch is dissolved. Add the remaining pan juices. Bring to a boil over medium heat and cook, stirring, until slightly thickened, about 5 minutes. Taste and adjust the seasonings. Pour into a warmed bowl.

Cut the loin into slices and arrange on a warmed platter. Serve the sauce alongside.

Serves 8

FOR THE STUFFING

2 tablespoons olive oil

$1 1/2$ cups (6 oz/185 g) chopped Golden Delicious or other baking apple

1 cup (4 oz/125 g) chopped yellow onion

1 clove garlic, finely chopped

$1/2$ cup ($1 1/2$ oz/45 g) finely chopped dried apples

$1/4$ cup ($1 1/2$ oz/45 g) raisins

$1/4$ teaspoon dried thyme

Salt and ground pepper to taste

$1/2$ cup (4 fl oz/125 ml) apple cider

1 boneless pork loin, $2 1/2$ lb (1.25 kg)

$1/4$ teaspoon dried thyme

Salt and ground pepper to taste

1 cup (8 fl oz/250 ml) apple cider, plus more as needed

2 teaspoons cornstarch (cornflour)

Baked Ham with Orange-Mustard-Pepper Glaze

A baked ham makes an impressive centerpiece for a buffet table. Depending on the occasion, serve it paired with your favorite side dishes or offer it sliced alongside a basket of warmed rolls and a dish of honey mustard for impromptu sandwiches.

Let the ham stand at room temperature for about 1 hour before baking. Preheat an oven to 325°F (165°C).

Unwrap the ham and wipe the surface with a damp paper towel. Trim off any extra-thick layers of fat. Score the outside surface of the ham in a diamond pattern, making crosscuts 1/2 inch (12 mm) apart.

Place the ham in a large roasting pan, rounded side up. Bake for 30 minutes.

Meanwhile, make the glaze: In a small bowl, stir together the orange marmalade, mustard, soy sauce, and pepper.

Remove the ham from the oven and spread half of the glaze over the surface of the ham. Return to the oven and bake, basting every 20 minutes with the remaining glaze until it is used up. The ham will take about 12–15 minutes per pound (500 g) and is done when an instant-read thermometer inserted into the thickest part registers 140°F (60°C), about 1 hour longer.

Remove from the oven and transfer the ham to a warmed platter. Cover loosely with aluminum foil. Let stand for 20 minutes before carving. Slice and arrange on the platter to serve.

Serves 8

1/2 fully cooked bone-in or boneless butt end ham, about 6 lb (3 kg)

FOR THE GLAZE

3/4 cup (7 1/2 oz/235 g) orange marmalade

1 tablespoon Dijon mustard

1 tablespoon soy sauce

1/2 teaspoon coarsely ground pepper

Venison Loin with Mushroom Sauce

1 boneless venison loin, 2–3 lb (1–1.5 kg)

1/2 cup (4 fl oz/125 ml) dry red wine

1/2 cup (2 oz/60 g) chopped shallots

6 juniper berries or 1 1/2 tablespoons gin

1 teaspoon coarsely ground pepper

FOR THE MUSHROOM SAUCE

2 cups (16 fl oz/500 ml) beef broth

1/2 cup (about 1 oz/30 g) dried porcini mushrooms

1/4 cup (2 oz/60 g) unsalted butter

3/4 lb (375 g) assorted fresh mushrooms such as shiitake, morel, chanterelle, white button, and cremini, in any combination, brushed clean and sliced

1 small clove garlic, finely chopped

1 teaspoon fresh thyme leaves

1/2 teaspoon snipped fresh rosemary

Salt and ground pepper to taste

Place the venison in a shallow baking dish. Add the wine, shallots, juniper berries or gin, and pepper. Turn to coat the meat on all sides. Cover and refrigerate for at least 12 hours, or for up to 24 hours.

The next day, make the mushroom sauce: In a saucepan over high heat, combine the beef broth and dried porcini. Bring to a boil, cover, reduce the heat to low, and simmer for 5 minutes. Remove from the heat and let stand for 20 minutes. Pour the mushrooms and broth through a fine-mesh sieve lined with dampened cheesecloth (muslin) placed over a bowl; reserve the liquid. If the porcini feel gritty, rinse with cold water. Squeeze dry and chop coarsely.

In a frying pan over medium-low heat, melt the butter. Add the fresh mushrooms and sauté until tender, about 10 minutes. Stir in the reserved porcini, garlic, thyme, rosemary, salt, and pepper. Cook, stirring, until hot, 1–2 minutes. Set aside.

Preheat an oven to 400°F (200°C). Lift the venison from the marinade, reserving the marinade. Pat dry with paper towels. Heat a heavy nonstick frying pan over medium heat. Add the venison and brown on all sides, about 6 minutes. Transfer to a roasting pan and roast 10–12 minutes for medium-rare. Transfer to a cutting board and cover with aluminum foil. Let rest while finishing the sauce.

Place the roasting pan over medium-high heat. Add the reserved marinade and deglaze the pan, stirring to dislodge any browned bits. Boil until reduced to 1/2 cup (4 fl oz/125 ml), about 5 minutes. Add the porcini liquid and boil until the mixture is reduced to 1 cup (8 fl oz/250 ml), about 5 minutes. Strain into the pan holding the sautéed mushrooms. Reheat and season with salt and pepper.

To serve, cut the venison across the grain into thin slices and arrange on a warmed platter. Using a slotted spoon, lift out the mushrooms and arrange on top of the meat. Pass the remaining sauce at the table.

Serves 8

Caramelized Veal Chops with Balsamic Syrup

An easy preparation with an impressive delivery, these veal chops can be regally accompanied with green beans tossed in sesame oil and sesame seeds and mashed sweet potatoes.

In a small saucepan over medium-high heat, combine the vinegar and soy sauce. Bring to a boil and boil until the liquid is reduced to 3 tablespoons, about 5 minutes. Remove from the heat, stir in the orange juice, and set aside.

In a small bowl, stir together the sugar and peppercorns. Press the sugar mixture onto one side of each veal chop, dividing it evenly.

Heat a large nonstick frying pan over medium-high heat. Coat the pan with nonstick cooking spray. Add the chops, sugar sides down, and cook until caramelized on the first side, about 2 minutes. Turn and continue to cook until pale pink when cut into at the thickest point, about 3 minutes longer.

Transfer the chops to a warmed platter. Return the pan to medium-high heat. Pour in the reduced vinegar mixture and deglaze the pan, stirring with a wooden spoon to remove any browned bits from the pan bottom. Bring to a boil and boil until the liquid is reduced to 3 tablespoons, about 3 minutes.

Streak warmed individual plates with the reduction and top with the veal. Serve hot.

Serves 4

1/3 cup (3 fl oz/80 ml) balsamic vinegar

2 tablespoons soy sauce

1/2 cup (4 fl oz/125 ml) orange juice

1 tablespoon sugar

2 teaspoons crushed white peppercorns

4 veal rib chops, 6 oz (185 g) each, trimmed of fat

Sautéed Veal with Prosciutto and Sage

This classic Italian preparation for veal is a perfect choice for a casual get together during the otherwise hectic holiday season. Skinless, boneless chicken breasts are an obvious alternative to the veal.

1¹/₂ lb (750 g) veal scallops (about 8 total), each ¹/₃–¹/₂ inch (9–12 mm) thick

Salt and ground pepper to taste

16 fresh sage leaves

8 thin slices prosciutto

3 tablespoons olive oil

¹/₂ cup (4 fl oz/125 ml) beef, veal, or rich chicken broth

¹/₂ cup (4 fl oz/125 ml) dry Marsala

¹/₄ cup (2 oz/60 g) unsalted butter, at room temperature, cut into slivers

One at a time, place the veal scallops between 2 sheets of plastic wrap and gently pound with a meat pounder until about ¹/₄ inch (6 mm) thick.

Sprinkle the veal lightly with salt and pepper, and top each piece with 2 sage leaves. Cover the sage leaves on each scallop with 1 slice prosciutto and secure in place with toothpicks.

In a sauté pan large enough to accommodate all the veal slices in a single layer (or using 2 pans), warm the olive oil over medium-high heat. Add the veal scallops and sauté until golden, about 3 minutes. Turn and sauté the second side until golden, 3–4 minutes longer. Transfer the veal to a warmed platter or individual plates, remove the toothpicks, and keep warm.

Return the pan to high heat. Pour in the broth and Marsala and deglaze the pan, stirring with a wooden spoon to remove any browned bits from the pan bottom. Reduce the pan juices until thickened, 8–10 minutes. Remove from the heat and swirl in the butter.

Spoon the pan juices over the veal and serve at once.

Serves 4

Herb-Crusted Beef Medallions with Red Wine Sauce

A rich-tasting but low-fat version of a restaurant-style dish, these beef medallions are coated with a crumb mixture made from panko, coarse dried bread crumbs used in Japanese cooking. If you like, serve with roasted Yukon gold potatoes.

In a heavy saucepan over medium heat, combine the shallots and wine. Bring to a boil and boil until the liquid has evaporated, about 20 minutes. Add the broth and boil until reduced to 3/4 cup (6 fl oz/180 ml), about 20 minutes longer. Remove from the heat and pour into a blender or food processor. Add the 2 tablespoons bread crumbs and the butter and purée to form a smooth sauce.

About 10 minutes before the sauce is ready, in a small bowl, stir together the remaining 1/2 cup (2 oz/60 g) bread crumbs, the parsley, thyme, sage, and egg white.

Heat a large frying pan over medium-high heat. Coat the pan with nonstick cooking spray. Season the beef medallions with salt and pepper and add to the pan. Sear, turning once, about 2 minutes on each side. Remove from the pan and press the herb mixture onto one side of each medallion.

Again coat the pan with cooking spray and return to medium-high heat. Return the medallions to the pan, crumb sides down, and cook until golden and the meat is medium-rare, about 2 minutes.

Remove from the heat. Ladle the puréed sauce onto warmed individual plates, dividing it evenly. Place the beef medallions, crumb sides up, on the sauce. Serve hot.

Serves 4

2 large shallots, chopped

1 cup (8 fl oz/250 ml) Zinfandel or other full-bodied red wine

2 cups (16 fl oz/500 ml) beef broth

2 tablespoons plus 1/2 cup (2 1/2 oz/75 g) panko bread crumbs (see note) or other coarse dried bread crumbs

1 teaspoon unsalted butter

3 tablespoons chopped fresh flat-leaf (Italian) parsley

1 tablespoon *each* chopped fresh thyme and sage

1 egg white

4 filets mignons, trimmed, each 5 oz (155 g) and 1 1/4 inches (3 cm) thick

Salt and ground pepper to taste

Osso Buco

This classic Milanese dish of braised veal shanks and sauteed vegetables can be ready for the oven in 40 minutes, but it does require at least 2 hours to simmer. At the butcher shop, ask for center-cut veal hind shanks cut into 2-inch rounds.

4 tablespoons unsalted butter, cut into pieces

3 leeks, white and pale green parts only, chopped

3 carrots, peeled and chopped

3 celery stalks, chopped

3 garlic cloves, minced

1 tablespoon minced fresh marjoram

1/4 cup (1/3 oz/10 g) finely chopped fresh parsley

1/3 cup (3 fl oz/80 ml) olive oil, or as needed

6 slices center-cut veal shank, each about 12 oz (375 g) and 2 inches (5 cm) thick

Salt and freshly ground pepper to taste

6 tablespoons all-purpose flour

2 cups (16 fl oz/500 ml) dry white wine

1 can (14 1/2 oz/455 g) finely diced plum (Italian) tomatoes

1 1/2 cups (12 fl oz/375 ml) chicken broth

Preheat an oven to 325°F (190°C).

In a large, heavy ovenproof Dutch oven or sauté pan over medium-low heat, melt the butter. Add the leeks, carrots, celery, garlic, marjoram, and 2 tablespoons of the parsley. Sauté, stirring often, until the vegetables are tender, about 15 minutes. Transfer the vegetables to a large heatproof dish, using a rubber spatula to remove all the remnants from the pan.

Return the pan to medium-high heat and add 2 tablespoons of the olive oil. Season the veal shanks with salt and pepper and coat lightly with the flour, shaking off the excess. Working in batches, brown the shanks on all sides, adding more oil as needed, 7–9 minutes total. Transfer the shanks to the dish with the vegetables. Pour off any fat in the pan and return the pan to the heat. Add the white wine and deglaze the pan, stirring with a wooden spoon to scrape up any browned bits from the bottom. Continue to simmer until the wine almost completely evaporates. Return the vegetables to the pan and arrange the shanks upright in a single layer over the top. Pour in the tomatoes and the broth and bring to a simmer over medium heat.

Once the liquid is simmering, cover the pan and bake in the oven until the veal is fork-tender and falling off the bone, about 2 hours. Taste and adjust the seasonings.

Carefully transfer the shanks to a warmed serving platter and spoon the sauce over and around them. Sprinkle with the remaining 2 tablespoons parsley. Serve at once.

Serves 6

Standing Rib Roast with Jerusalem Artichokes

A standing rib roast is one of the most celebratory of all holiday dishes. Here, side dishes are made simple by roasting vegetables in the same pan. If you can't find jerusalem artichokes, substitute them with any of your favorite root vegetables.

In a small bowl, stir together the rosemary, thyme, garlic, 1 teaspoon coarse salt, and $1/2$ teaspoon pepper. Place the roast, rib side down, in a large roasting pan. Rub half of the herb mixture over the meat. Let stand for 30 minutes.

Preheat an oven to 475°F (245°C). Roast for 20 minutes. Remove from the oven and, using a bulb baster, transfer most of the rendered fat to a measuring cup; set aside. Reduce the oven temperature to 350°F (180°C) and continue to roast for 30 minutes.

Meanwhile, in a bowl, toss together the potatoes, shallots, and about $1/4$ cup (2 fl oz/60 ml) of the reserved fat. (Discard the remaining fat.) Sprinkle with salt and pepper.

When the meat has roasted for 50 minutes, add the potatoes and shallots to the pan and continue to roast for 30 minutes. Add the Jerusalem artichokes, and sprinkle all the vegetables with the remaining herb mixture. Continue to roast until an instant-read thermometer inserted into the thickest part of the roast away from the bone registers 125°–130°F (52°–54°C) for medium-rare, 30–45 minutes longer.

Transfer the roast to a warmed platter. Cover with aluminum foil and let stand for 20 minutes. Transfer the vegetables to a dish and keep warm. Pour the pan juices into a cup and spoon off most of the fat. Return the juices to the pan, along with the wine and broth. Place over medium-high heat, bring to a boil, and deglaze the pan, stirring to dislodge any browned bits. Continue to cook until reduced by one-half, about 15 minutes. Strain into a small pitcher. Season to taste with salt and pepper.

Carve the meat into slices. Serve the juices and vegetables at the table.

Serves 12–14

2 teaspoons dried rosemary

1 teaspoon dried thyme

2 cloves garlic, lightly crushed

1 teaspoon coarse salt, plus salt to taste

$1/2$ teaspoon ground pepper, plus pepper to taste

3-rib standing rib roast, about $8^{1}/_2$ lb (4.25 kg)

10–12 Yukon gold or other yellow-fleshed potatoes ($2^{1}/_2$–3 lb/1.25–1.5 kg total weight), peeled and halved

1 lb (500 g) shallots (about 24), peeled but left whole

2 lb (1 kg) Jerusalem artichokes, unpeeled

1 cup (8 fl oz/250 ml) full-bodied red wine such as Cabernet Sauvignon or Merlot

1 cup (8 fl oz/250 ml) beef broth

FOR THE MARINADE

4 cloves garlic, crushed

3 *each* fresh parsley sprigs and fresh thyme springs

2 orange zest strips

12 *each* peppercorns and whole cloves

2 allspice berries

1 cinnamon stick

1 bottle (24 fl oz/750 ml) red wine

$1/4$ cup (2 fl oz/60 ml) olive oil

2 yellow onions, chopped

$2^{1}/_{2}$ lb (1.25 kg) boneless stewing beef, cut into cubes

$1/4$ cup (2 fl oz/60 ml) olive oil

2 cups (12 oz/375 g) peeled, seeded, and chopped tomatoes

$3/_4$ lb (375 g) carrots, peeled and thickly sliced

$1/_8$ cup ($3^{1}/_{2}$ oz/105 g) pitted brine-cured black olives

Salt and ground pepper to taste

Chopped fresh thyme to taste

Hearty Beef Stew

To make the marinade, combine the garlic, parsley, thyme, orange zest, peppercorns, cloves, allspice, and cinnamon stick on a square of cheesecloth (muslin). Bring the corners together and tie securely with kitchen string. Pour the wine and $1/4$ cup (2 fl oz/60 ml) olive oil into a deep nonaluminum container and add the onions and cheesecloth bag. Add the beef to the marinade, stir, cover, and refrigerate for 24 hours.

Preheat an oven to 300°F (150°C). Remove the meat from the marinade and pat dry. Reserve the marinade. In a heavy sauté pan over high heat, warm half of the olive oil. Brown half of the meat on all sides, 5–10 minutes. Transfer the browned meat to a heavy pot. Add the remaining oil to the pan and brown the remaining meat. Add it to the pot. Add the reserved marinade, including the cheesecloth bag, and the tomatoes. Add water as needed just to cover. Cover, bring to a boil over high heat, transfer to the oven, and bake until meltingly tender, 3–4 hours.

While the beef is cooking, bring a saucepan three-fourths full of salted water to a boil. Add the carrots and cook until tender when pierced with a knife, about 10 minutes. Drain and set aside.

When the beef is tender, remove from the oven and discard the cheesecloth bag. Using a large spoon, skim off the excess fat from the surface. Add the carrots and olives and place over medium heat until hot. Season with salt and pepper.

Transfer to a warmed serving bowl. Sprinkle with chopped thyme and serve.

Serves 4

Beef Brisket with Sweet Onions

Preheat an oven to 325°F (165°C). Salt and pepper the brisket on all sides. In a large, wide ovenproof pan with a tight-fitting lid, warm the olive oil over medium-high heat. Add the brisket and brown well on both sides, about 6 minutes total. Transfer to a plate. Add the onion and carrot to the pan and sauté until golden, about 5 minutes. Add the garlic and sauté for 1 minute. Add the tomatoes and juices, 1 cup (8 fl oz/250 ml) of the wine, and the bay leaf. Mix well and bring to a boil. Return the brisket to the pan, cover, and place in the oven.

Cook, basting occasionally with the pan juices, until tender, about 3 hours. Remove from the oven and let cool in the juices. Transfer the brisket to a deep platter. Cover with aluminum foil and refrigerate until cold, at least 2 hours or up to overnight. Let the pan juices cool, then strain into a bowl and set aside. Discard the solids.

Just before serving, preheat the oven to 350°F (180°C). Cut the brisket across the grain into thin slices. Arrange the slices on an ovenproof serving platter. Cover with aluminum foil and place in the oven for 15 minutes to heat through.

Meanwhile, cook the onions: In a large frying pan over medium-low heat, warm the olive oil. Add the onions and sauté, stirring often, until golden brown, about 20 minutes. Season with salt and pepper. While the onions are cooking, pour the remaining 1 cup (8 fl oz/250 ml) wine into a saucepan. Add ¼ cup (1 oz/30 g) of the dried cherries and bring to a boil over high heat. Boil until reduced by one-half, about 5 minutes. Stir in the puréed brisket juices and return to a boil. Season to taste with salt and pepper.

To serve, remove the brisket from the oven. Pour the sauce evenly over the top. Spoon the onions and the remaining ¼ cup (1 oz/30 g) dried cherries over the sauce. Carve into slices at the table, spooning onions and sauce over each serving.

Serves 8

Salt and ground pepper
to taste

1 first or flat cut brisket,
4–5 lb (2–2.5 kg)

2 tablespoons olive oil

1½ cups (6 oz/185 g) chopped
yellow onion

½ cup (2½ oz/75 g) diced
carrot

2 cloves garlic, finely chopped

1 can (28 oz/875 g) plum
(Roma) tomatoes, with juices

2 cups (16 fl oz/500 ml) Merlot
or other full-bodied red wine

1 bay leaf

FOR THE ONIONS

2 tablespoons olive oil

3 cups (10½ oz/330 g) thinly
sliced sweet onions such as
Vidalia

Salt and ground pepper to
taste

½ cup (2 oz/60 g) pitted dried
cherries

Pepper-and-Cumin-Coated Lamb Chops

A dry rub of just three ingredients—coarsely ground pepper, cumin, and salt—adds hearty flavor to lamb. Cooked on a stove-top grill pan, these chops are a quick and easy way to "grill" during the colder months.

1½ tablespoons cumin seeds

1 tablespoon coarsely ground pepper

1½ teaspoons kosher salt

18 rib lamb chops, about 4 oz (125 g) each, trimmed of fat

2–3 teaspoons olive oil

Fresh mint sprigs (optional)

Place the cumin seeds in a small lock-top plastic bag and crush coarsely using a meat pounder or rolling pin. Place the crushed seeds in a small bowl and add the pepper and kosher salt. Mix well.

Pat the chops dry, then pat $^1/_4$ teaspoon of seasoning mixture on each side of each chop. Place the chops on a baking sheet, cover with aluminum foil, and refrigerate for 30 minutes.

When ready to cook, brush a stove-top grill pan lightly with olive oil and place over medium heat. When hot, add enough chops to fit comfortably in a single layer and cook on one side until brown and crusty, about 3 minutes. Turn and cook until brown and crusty on the second side but still pink in the center when cut into with a sharp knife, about 3 minutes longer. Transfer to a warmed platter and cover loosely with aluminum foil. Repeat with the remaining chops until all are cooked, brushing the pan with more oil as needed to prevent sticking.

Garnish with a small bouquet of fresh mint, if desired. Serve at once.

Serves 6

Lamb Chops with Moroccan Spices

Earthy, pungent, hot, and sweet spices are highlighted in this flavorful alternative to more classic lamb preparations. Serve the chops with couscous and sautéed beets and carrots glazed with butter, orange juice and zest, and a hint of mint.

In a small bowl, stir together the $^1/_2$ cup ($^3/_4$ oz/20 g) mint, the coriander, garlic, paprika, cumin, black pepper, cayenne pepper, salt, lemon juice, and olive oil. Rub the mixture into the chops, coating evenly, and place in a nonaluminum container. Cover and marinate at cool room temperature for 2 hours or for up to overnight in the refrigerator.

Prepare a fire in a charcoal or gas grill. If the chops are refrigerated, bring to room temperature.

Place the chops on an oiled grill rack and grill, turning once, for 4 minutes on each side for medium-rare, or until done to your liking.

Transfer to a warmed platter or individual plates and sprinkle with mint, if using. Serve at once.

Serves 4

$^1/_2$ cup ($^3/_4$ oz/20 g) chopped fresh mint, plus extra for garnish (optional)

1 tablespoon ground coriander

2 teaspoons finely minced garlic

1 teaspoon sweet paprika

1 teaspoon ground cumin

1 teaspoon ground black pepper

$^1/_4$ teaspoon cayenne pepper

Salt to taste

Juice of 1 lemon

2 tablespoons olive oil

8 loin lamb chops or 16 small rib chops

Rosemary Lamb Chops

Accompany these rosemary-infused lamb chops with classic scalloped potatoes, or try the Sweet and White Potato Gratin (page 217) for an interesting variation. If you like, cook the chops on a charcoal grill instead of broiling them.

12 loin lamb chops, about ¼ lb (125g) each

6 tablespoons (3 fl oz/90 ml) olive oil

1½ tablespoons minced fresh rosemary

6 garlic cloves, thinly sliced

Ground pepper and salt to taste

Place the lamb chops a shallow dish large enough to hold them in a single layer. Add the olive oil, rosemary, garlic, and pepper. Turn the chops to coat them with the seasonings. Let stand at room temperature to marinate for 1 hour.

Position a rack in a broiler (griller) about 6 inches from the heat source and preheat the broiler. Working in 2 batches if necessary, transfer the lamb chops to a broiler pan without crowding, leaving the garlic behind. Season with salt. Broil for 4 minutes, then turn, season with salt, and broil on the second side until done to your liking, about 3 minutes longer for medium-rare.

Transfer the lamb chops to a warmed serving platter or individual dinner plates.

Serves 6

Vegetables & Side Dishes

Terrine of Winter Kale and Yukon Gold Potatoes with Sausage

The flavors here are similar to those of *caldo verde*, the famous Portuguese soup also made with kale, potatoes, and sausage. Since this hearty casserole is especially delicious when made ahead, it's a good choice for a weekend with guests.

1 clove garlic, lightly crushed

6½ tablespoons (3½ oz/105 g) unsalted butter

½ lb (250 g) spicy chicken sausages, casings removed

2–2½ lb (1–1.25 kg) Yukon gold or red or white new potatoes, unpeeled, thinly sliced

Salt and ground pepper to taste

1 bunch kale, trimmed and coarsely chopped

2 oz (60 g) Monterey jack cheese, shredded

½ cup (4 fl oz/125 ml) milk

Preheat an oven to 350°F (180°C). Rub the bottom and sides of a 2- to 2½-qt (2- to 2.5-l) rectangular baking dish with the garlic, then grease it with about ½ tablespoon of the butter.

Crumble the sausage into a frying pan and cook over medium heat, stirring occasionally, until lightly browned, 5–7 minutes. Using a slotted spoon, transfer to paper towels to drain.

Cut the remaining 6 tablespoons (3 oz/90 g) butter into bits. Make a layer of one-third of the potato slices, overlapping slightly, in the bottom and along the sides of the prepared baking dish. Dot with about one-fourth of the butter and sprinkle with salt and pepper. Top with one-third of the crumbled sausage, one-third of the kale, and one-third of the cheese. Repeat the layers twice, ending with a layer of cheese. Dot with the remaining butter, then pour the milk evenly over the top. Cover the dish tightly with aluminum foil.

Bake until the potatoes are very tender when pierced with a knife, about 1 hour. Remove from the oven and let stand for about 10 minutes.

To serve, run a knife along the sides of the terrine and invert it onto a cutting board. Cut into slices 1½–2 inches (4–5 cm) thick and transfer to warmed individual plates. Serve immediately.

Serves 4–6

Butternut Squash Risotto

This risotto, made with Italian medium-grain rice, is packed into individual ramekins and unmolded onto small mounds of butternut squash purée. Accompanied by a salad, it makes a memorable harvest time or holiday luncheon.

Preheat an oven to 375°F (190°C). Line a baking sheet with parchment (baking) paper. Cut the butternut squash in half through the stem end and discard the seeds and fibers. Place the squash halves, cut sides down, on the prepared baking sheet. Bake until softened, 20–25 minutes. Let cool. Meanwhile, pour the broth into a saucepan and bring to a boil. Reduce the heat to maintain a gentle simmer.

Scoop out the pulp from the cooled squash halves and place in a food processor with $1/4$ cup (2 fl oz/60 ml) of the broth. Purée until smooth. Transfer to a saucepan and add the parsley and nutmeg. Season with salt and pepper. Cover to keep warm, adding a little broth if the purée begins to dry out.

In a saucepan over medium heat, warm the olive oil. Add the onion and sauté until softened, about 3 minutes. Add the rice, stir to coat with the oil, and cook, stirring, until the edges are translucent, 3–4 minutes. Add a ladleful of the simmering broth and continue to stir constantly over medium heat. When the broth is almost fully absorbed, add another ladleful. Continue to stir and add more broth, a ladleful at a time, as soon as each ladleful is almost absorbed. The risotto is done when the rice is tender but firm, about 20 minutes total. Stir in $1/4$ cup (2 oz/60 g) of the squash purée and season with salt and pepper.

Divide the remaining squash purée among 6 individual plates. Working quickly, spoon about 1 cup of the risotto into a 1-cup (8–fl oz/250-ml) ramekin, packing it tightly. Unmold the risotto on top of the squash purée. Repeat with the remaining risotto to make 6 servings. Garnish with chopped parsley and serve.

Serves 6

1 lb (500 g) butternut squash

$7^{1}/_{2}$–8 cups (60–64 fl oz/ 1.9–2 l) vegetable broth

2 tablespoons minced fresh flat-leaf (Italian) parsley, plus chopped parsley for garnish

$1/4$ teaspoon ground nutmeg

Salt and ground pepper to taste

$1/4$ cup (2 fl oz/60 ml) extra-virgin olive oil

1 yellow onion, diced

$1^{1}/_{2}$ cups ($10^{1}/_{2}$ oz/330 g) Carnaroli or Arborio rice

Winter White Lasagne

1 butternut squash, 1½ lb (750 g), halved lengthwise and seeds and fibers removed

12 dried lasagne noodles

6 tablespoons (3 oz/90 g) unsalted butter

6 tablespoons (2 oz/60 g) all–purpose (plain) flour

3 cups (24 fl oz/750 ml) half-and-half (half cream), heated

½ cup (2 oz/60 g) grated Parmesan cheese

¼ teaspoon grated nutmeg

Salt and ground pepper to taste

2 cups (1 lb/500 g) ricotta cheese

½ cup (2 oz/60 g) grated pecorino romano cheese

2 eggs

¾ cup (1 oz/30 g) chopped fresh flat-leaf (Italian) parsley

Pinch of ground cloves

2 tablespoons olive oil

14 oz (440 g) fresh mushrooms, brushed clean and sliced

2 cloves garlic, finely chopped

1 cup (5 oz/155 g) crumbled Gorgonzola cheese

2 cups (8 oz/250 g) shredded fontina cheese

Preheat an oven to 350°F (180°C). Place the squash halves, cut sides down, in a baking pan and add a few spoonfuls of water. Cover and bake until tender, about 35 minutes. Let cool, then peel and cut crosswise into thin slices. Set aside.

Meanwhile, bring a large pot three-fourths full of salted water to a boil over high heat. Add the noodles, stir, and cook until just al dente, about 10 minutes or as per the package directions. Drain and immerse in cold water until ready to use.

Meanwhile, in a saucepan over low heat, melt the butter. Add the flour and cook, stirring, for 2 minutes. Gradually stir in the hot half-and-half and bring to a boil over low heat. Boil gently, stirring constantly, until thickened, about 5 minutes. Stir in the Parmesan cheese, nutmeg, salt, and pepper. Set aside. In a bowl, whisk together the ricotta and romano cheeses, eggs, ½ cup (⅛ oz/20 g) of the parsley, cloves, and pepper to taste. Set aside.

In a frying pan over medium-high heat, warm the olive oil. Add the mushrooms and cook, stirring, until lightly browned, about 10 minutes. Add the remaining ¼ cup (⅓ oz/10 g) parsley, garlic, and salt and pepper to taste. Cook, stirring, for 2 minutes. Remove from the heat and set aside.

If the oven has been turned off, reheat it to 350°F (180°C). Lightly butter a shallow 10-by-14-inch (25-by-35-cm) baking dish. Drain the noodles and pat dry with paper towels. Arrange 4 noodles, slightly overlapping, on the bottom of the prepared dish. Spread with the ricotta mixture and top with a layer of the squash slices. Add a second layer of noodles. Top with a layer of the mushrooms. Sprinkle with the Gorgonzola cheese. Top with a final layer of noodles. Pour the béchamel sauce over the top. Sprinkle evenly with the fontina cheese.

Bake until the top is browned and bubbly, 45–55 minutes. Remove from the oven and let stand for 15 minutes. Cut into squares to serve.

Serves 8–10

Jerusalem Artichokes with Bacon and Balsamic

Although Jerusalem artichokes have a nutty, potatolike flavor, they have a crisper texture than potatoes. Look for them during the winter months in farmers' markets and other well-stocked markets.

Using a vegetable peeler or paring knife, peel the Jerusalem artichokes. Then using a mandoline or sharp knife, cut into paper-thin slices. Set aside.

In a frying pan over medium heat, cook the bacon, turning as needed, until crisp, about 5 minutes. Using a slotted spoon, transfer to paper towels to drain.

If the bacon rendered any fat, pour off all but 1 teaspoon of the bacon fat from the pan. Add the olive oil to the pan and return to medium heat. When the oil is hot, add the Jerusalem artichokes, onion, roasted garlic, if using, and pepper. Sauté, stirring often, until the onion is translucent and the Jerusalem artichokes are tender to the bite but not soft, 4–5 minutes.

Transfer the contents of the frying pan to a serving bowl, then return the pan to medium heat. Pour in the vinegar and water and deglaze the pan, stirring to dislodge any browned bits from the pan bottom. Add the contents of the pan to the bowl. Add the bacon and toss gently to mix. Serve immediately.

Serves 4

1 lb (500 g) Jerusalem artichokes

2 or 3 slices Canadian bacon, about 2 oz (60 g) total weight, finely diced

1 tablespoon extra-virgin olive oil

3 tablespoons minced yellow onion

3 cloves roasted garlic, halved (optional)

1/2 teaspoon ground pepper

2 tablespoons balsamic vinegar

1 teaspoon water

Haricots Verts with Toasted Almond Butter

Haricots verts are small, slender, very tender French green beans. The toasted almond butter adds a festive touch. Try it with any of your favorite vegetables, including broccoli, broccolini, cauliflower, or even leafy greens such as spinach or chard.

1 cup (3½ oz/105 g) sliced (flaked) almonds

3 tablespoons cold unsalted butter, cut into pieces

2 teaspoons grated lemon zest

2 lb (1 kg) haricots verts or other slender green beans, stem ends trimmed

1 tablespoon kosher or coarse salt, plus salt to taste

Freshly ground pepper to taste

In a dry frying pan over medium-low heat, toast the almonds, stirring often, until golden brown, about 5 minutes. Remove from the heat and let cool.

Transfer the almonds to a food processor and pulse to chop finely. With the motor running, add the butter pieces and lemon zest and process just until blended. Scrape into a small bowl and set aside.

Bring a large pot three-fourths full of water to a boil over high heat. Stir in the beans and the 1 tablespoon salt. Cook, stirring occasionally, until the beans are tender but still bright green, 3–5 minutes; the timing will depend upon the size of the beans. Drain immediately.

Transfer to a warmed serving bowl. Dot with the almond butter and toss to coat. Sprinkle with a little coarse salt and add a grinding of pepper. Serve immediately.

Serves 6–8

Artichokes Stewed with Lemon and Garlic

Artichokes prepared in this fashion—with lemon, bay, and garlic—are a classic Greek *meze*, or appetizer. They are also perfect as a side dish and, because they are served at room temperature, can be made ahead and left to marinate before serving.

Using a vegetable peeler, remove the zest from the lemons and set aside.

Fill a large bowl three-fourths full with water. Halve 1 lemon and squeeze the juice into the water. Working with 1 artichoke at a time, break off the tough outer leaves to reach the pale green, tender inner leaves. Trim away the tough, dark green layer around the base. Cut off the top one-half of the artichoke, including all of the prickly leaf points. Trim off the end of the stem, then pare the stem to reveal the light green center. Cut the artichoke in half lengthwise and slip the halves into the lemon water. Trim the remaining artichokes in the same way.

Drain the artichokes and place them in a saucepan. Halve the remaining 3 lemons and squeeze the juice into the saucepan. Add the reserved lemon zest, the garlic, thyme sprigs, bay leaves, salt, and olive oil. Add water just to cover and place a piece of parchment (baking) paper the diameter of the pan on top of the artichokes. Weight the parchment with a heatproof plate that rests directly on the artichokes. Bring to a boil over medium-high heat, reduce the heat to medium, and simmer for 5 minutes. Remove from the heat and let cool completely in the pan, about 1 hour or until tender when pierced with a knife.

Using a slotted spoon, transfer the artichokes to a bowl. Garnish with the parsley and serve at room temperature.

Makes 2 qt (2 l); serves 12

4 lemons

36 small artichokes, 1–2 oz (30–60 g) each

20 cloves garlic, halved

10 fresh thyme sprigs

5 bay leaves

1 1/2 teaspoons coarse salt

3/4 cup (6 fl oz/180 ml) olive oil

1 teaspoon chopped fresh flat-leaf (Italian) parsley

Escarole Soufflé

This impressive dish works equally well a side dish, first course, or as a main course accompanied by a light soup or salad. Escarole, a member of the chicory family, is at its peak in autumn and winter. Other bitter greens can be used in its place.

1½ tablespoons unsalted butter, melted, plus 2 tablespoons unsalted butter

3 tablespoons finely grated Parmesan cheese

3 tablespoons extra-virgin olive oil

2 leeks, white part only, thinly sliced

2 cups (4 oz/125 g) finely shredded escarole (Batavian endive), (see note)

2 tablespoons all-purpose (plain) flour

¾ cup (6 fl oz/180 ml) vegetable broth

¼ teaspoon cayenne pepper

Salt and ground black pepper to taste

3 eggs, separated

Preheat an oven to 350°F (180°C). Brush a 1-qt (1-l) soufflé dish with the 1½ tablespoons melted butter. Coat with the Parmesan cheese, tapping out the excess.

In a sauté pan over medium heat, warm the olive oil. Add the leeks and sauté until softened, 5–7 minutes. Add the shredded escarole and sauté until tender, 3–4 minutes longer. Remove from the heat and set aside to cool.

In a saucepan over medium heat, melt the 2 tablespoons butter. Add the flour and cook, stirring, until well incorporated, 3–4 minutes. Slowly add the broth while whisking constantly. Bring to a boil, reduce the heat to low and cook, stirring, until thickened, 5–6 minutes. Add the cayenne pepper, salt, and black pepper. Let cool.

In a large bowl, combine the cooled escarole-leek mixture and the flour-broth mixture. Add the egg yolks and stir with a large spoon to mix well. In a bowl, beat the egg whites until stiff peaks form. Stir about one-third of the whites into the escarole mixture to lighten it. Then fold in the remaining egg whites just until no white streaks remain.

Pour into the prepared soufflé dish and place the dish in a large baking pan. Pour hot water into the baking pan to reach halfway up the sides of the soufflé dish. Bake for 10 minutes. Remove the baking pan and soufflé dish from the oven. Reduce the oven temperature to 325°F (160°C). Return the soufflé dish to the oven and bake until the soufflé rises nicely and is lightly browned, 18–20 minutes longer.

Serves 6

Chard, Spinach, and Mushroom Gratin

The topping of bread crumbs and Parmesan cheese turns a rich golden brown in the oven, complementing the earthy flavors of the greens and mushrooms in this robust casserole. You can also offer this dish as a vegetarian main course.

Preheat an oven to 325°F (165°C). Butter a shallow 1-qt (1-l) baking dish.

In a large nonstick frying pan over medium heat, melt 2 tablespoons of the butter. Add the shallot and mushrooms and sauté until softened, about 2 minutes. Stir in the mustard and sauté for 10 seconds longer. Stir in the water and vinegar. Add the chard and spinach, a handful at a time, waiting for each handful to wilt before adding the next one. It should take about 30 seconds for each addition to wilt. When all of the greens have been added, season with salt and pepper and remove from the heat.

Transfer to the prepared baking dish. Sprinkle the bread crumbs and cheese evenly over the top and then drizzle evenly with the oil. Dot with the remaining 2 tablespoons butter.

Bake until heated through and the top is golden brown, 15–20 minutes. Remove from the oven and serve directly from the dish.

Serves 4–6

4 tablespoons (2 oz/60 g) unsalted butter

1 shallot, minced

6 oz (185 g) fresh cremini mushrooms, brushed clean and sliced, or portobello mushrooms, brushed clean and chopped

1½ teaspoons dry mustard

½ cup (4 fl oz/125 ml) water

2 tablespoons red wine vinegar

1 small bunch red or green Swiss chard, about 6 oz (185 g), trimmed and coarsely chopped

1 bunch spinach, about ¾ lb (375 g), tough stems removed and coarsely chopped

Salt and ground pepper to taste

⅓ cup (1½ oz/45 g) fine dried bread crumbs

3–4 tablespoons grated Parmesan cheese

1 tablespoon olive oil

Asparagus with Butter and Lemon

Asparagus is one of the first green vegetables of springtime, making it a favorite choice for spring holiday suppers. If you like, sprinkle the asparagus with a little chopped fresh flat-leaf (Italian) parsley just before serving.

20 asparagus spears

1 teaspoon salt

3 tablespoons unsalted butter

1 lemon, cut into quarters

Snap off the tough end of each asparagus spear, then trim away any ragged edges on the base. If the spears are young and slender, they do not need to be peeled. If they are mature and stocky, using a vegetable peeler, peel each spear to within about 1 inch (2.5 cm) of the tip. Divide the asparagus into 4 equal bundles, and tie each bundle together with kitchen string. Set the bundles aside.

Fill a wide, shallow saucepan three-fourths full with water and bring to a rapid boil over high heat. Add the salt and then carefully lower the aspagus bundles into the boiling water. Boil the asparagus, uncovered, until tender when pierced with a knife tip, 4–6 minutes, depending on the size of the spears.

Meanwhile, in a small saucepan over low heat, melt the butter and keep hot. Using tongs, transfer the asparagus bundles to a cloth napkin or paper towels to drain for a few seconds, and then to a serving platter. Snip and discard the strings.

Pour the butter over the top of the asparagus. Pass the lemon wedges at the table.

Serves 4

Fava Beans with Pancetta and Lemon

Fava beans grow inside thick pods and have a rich, buttery flavor. Shell them as you would peas by first snapping off the stem and pulling away the tough string on the side of the pod. Then pop each pod open by pressing your thumbnails along its seam.

Bring a saucepan three-fourths full of water to a boil. Add the fava beans and cook for 3 minutes. Drain the beans. When cool enough to handle, split the translucent skin covering each bean and pop the bean free of the skin. Set the beans aside.

In a heavy frying pan over medium heat, sauté the pancetta until crisp, about 3 minutes. Add the carrot and sauté until tender, about 5 minutes.

Stir in the fava beans, lemon zest, and sage, mixing well. Season with salt and pepper. Transfer to a warmed serving dish and serve hot.

Serves 4

2¼ lb (1.1 kg) fava (broad) beans, shelled

2 thin slices pancetta, chopped

1 large carrot, peeled and thinly sliced

1½ teaspoons minced lemon zest

1 teaspoon chopped fresh sage

Salt and ground pepper to taste

Pan-Roasted Shallots with Sherry Wine Glaze

Shallots are a delicious alternative to the old-fashioned pearl onions that are typically part of a holiday meal. They are available in many sizes, but larger ones are easier to peel, cutting the preparation time of this dish to a minimum.

2 lb (1 kg) shallots, halved lengthwise if large

2 tablespoons olive oil

2 teaspoons dried sage

$^1/_2$ teaspoon salt, plus salt to taste

Freshly ground pepper to taste

$^3/_4$ cup (6 fl oz/180 ml) sweet sherry

Fresh sage leaves (optional)

Preheat an oven to 400°F (200°C).

In a 10-inch (25-cm) pie dish or baking dish, combine the shallots, olive oil, 1 teaspoon of the dried sage, $^1/_2$ teaspoon salt, and a grinding of pepper. Toss to mix well. Roast, stirring once or twice, until the shallots are tender and golden, about 45 minutes.

About 5 minutes before the shallots are done, pour the sherry into a small frying pan and bring to a boil over medium-high heat. Boil gently until reduced by one-half, about 5 minutes.

Remove the dish from the oven, sprinkle the remaining 1 teaspoon dried sage over the sizzling shallots, and pour the reduced sherry on top. Season to taste with salt and pepper and toss to coat. Transfer to a serving dish. Garnish with fresh sage, if desired. Serve immediately.

Serves 4–6

Ginger-Glazed Vegetables

Julienne strips of zucchini, red bell pepper, and daikon quickly sautéed and aromatic with ginger make a light accompaniment to roast meat and fish. Daikon, a large Asian radish with crisp flesh, can be found in Asian markets and well-stocked food stores.

In a frying pan over medium-high heat, warm the oil. Add the zucchini, bell pepper, daikon, ginger, garlic, and sugar and sauté until the vegetables are wilted, 1–2 minutes. Add the water and cook until the vegetables are tender, about 5 minutes.

Raise the heat to high and boil until the liquid evaporates and the sugar and the other ingredients have caramelized to a shiny glaze, about 4 minutes. Season with salt and pepper.

Transfer to a warmed serving bowl. Garnish with the parsley, if desired, and serve immediately.

Serves 4–6

2 tablespoons safflower oil

1 zucchini (courgette), julienned

1 large red bell pepper (capsicum), seeded and julienned

1 daikon, about 1/4 lb (125 g), peeled and julienned

1 tablespoon peeled and chopped fresh ginger

2 cloves garlic, minced

1 teaspoon sugar

1/2 cup (4 fl oz/125 ml) water

Salt and ground black or white pepper

1/4 cup (1/3 oz/10 g) chopped fresh flat-leaf (Italian) parsley (optional)

Braised Red Cabbage with Apple and Currants

Cabbage with apples is traditionally served with pork or ham. For this holiday version, use red cabbage, which will cook to a brilliant fuchsia color. The dried currants, apple, and sugar add a touch of sweetness, while the vinegar contributes a mildly sour bite.

¼ cup (2 fl oz/60 ml) olive oil

1 head red cabbage, (about 2 lb/1 kg), cored and thinly sliced

1 Golden Delicious or other firm cooking apple, cored, peeled, and diced

¼ cup (1½ oz/45 g) dried currants or raisins

½ cup (4 fl oz/125 ml) aged cider vinegar, or to taste

2 tablespoons sugar

1 teaspoon salt, plus salt to taste

Freshly ground pepper to taste

2 tablespoons fresh flat-leaf (Italian) parsley leaves (optional)

In a large, deep sauté pan over medium heat, warm the olive oil. Add the cabbage, apple, and currants or raisins and stir to coat. Cover and cook until the cabbage is tender-crisp, about 10 minutes.

Uncover and sprinkle with $^1/_4$ cup (2 fl oz/60 ml) of the vinegar, the sugar, and 1 teaspoon salt. Cook, stirring, until the cabbage is tender, about 8 minutes longer. Taste and adjust the seasonings with vinegar, salt, and a grinding of pepper.

Remove from the heat and toss in the parsley, if using. Transfer to a warmed serving bowl and serve immediately.

Serves 8

Baked Acorn Squash with Maple Cream

In this delicous seasonal recipe, the maple syrup heightens the natural sweetness of the squash, while the cream adds a note of richness. Serve as a side dish to baked ham or roast poultry.

2 small acorn squashes

4 teaspoons unsalted butter, melted

Salt and freshly ground pepper to taste

¼ cup (3 oz/90 g) maple syrup

¼ cup (2 fl oz/60 ml) heavy (double) cream

Preheat the oven to 350°F (180°C).

Halve the squashes lengthwise and scoop out and discard the seeds and fibers. Cut a thin slice from the skin side of each half so that it will sit upright, and put the halves, hollow side up, in a baking dish that will hold them without crowding. Brush the cut side of each half with 1 teaspoon of the butter, then sprinkle with salt and pepper. In a small bowl, stir together the maple syrup and cream. Spoon 2 tablespoons of the mixture into the hollow of each squash half.

Bake until the squash halves are tender when pierced with a fork, about 1 hour. Transfer to individual plates or a platter and serve immediately.

Serves 4

Parmesan Cornmeal Spoon Bread

Spoon bread is a cross between a firm soufflé and a soft quick bread. It puffs up when hot and deflates slightly as it cools. This creamy variation on a classic of the American South is a delicious alternative to rice or potatoes.

Preheat an oven to 375°F (190°C). Lightly butter eight $1/2$-cup (4–fl oz/125-ml) individual soufflé dishes.

In a frying pan over medium-low heat, melt the butter. Add the onion and bell pepper and sauté until the onion is golden, about 5 minutes. Stir in the garlic and cook until softened, about 1 minute. Remove from the heat and set aside to cool.

Pour the milk into a saucepan, place over medium heat, and bring just to a boil. Meanwhile, pour the water into a bowl and gradually stir in the cornmeal until smooth. When the milk has come to a boil, add the cornmeal mixture and cook, stirring, over medium heat, until thick, about 5 minutes. Stir in the Parmesan, $3/4$ teaspoon salt, and the cayenne pepper. Remove from the heat and let cool for about 15 minutes.

Meanwhile, in a large bowl, whisk the egg yolks until blended. Gradually stir the cooled cornmeal mixture and the cooled onion mixture into the yolks until blended.

In a separate bowl, combine the egg whites and a pinch of salt and whisk or beat with an electric mixer until soft peaks form. Using a rubber spatula, fold the egg whites into the cornmeal-onion mixture just until blended. Spoon into the prepared dishes, dividing it evenly.

Bake until the tops are slightly puffed and browned, about 30 minutes. Serve immediately.

Serves 8

1 tablespoon unsalted butter

$1/2$ cup ($2^{1/2}$ oz/75 g) finely chopped yellow onion

$1/4$ cup ($1^{1/2}$ oz/45 g) minced red bell pepper (capsicum)

1 clove garlic, crushed

1 cup (8 fl oz/250 ml) milk

$1^{3/4}$ cups (14 fl oz/430 ml) water

$3/4$ cup (4 oz/125 g) yellow cornmeal

$2/3$ cup ($2^{1/2}$ oz/75 g) grated Italian Parmesan cheese

$3/4$ teaspoon salt, plus pinch of salt

$1/8$ teaspoon cayenne pepper

3 eggs, separated

Mixed Rice Pilaf with Dried Cherries and Apricots

The trademark of a true pilaf is that the rice (or other grain) is always first sautéed in butter before the broth is added. This colorful pilaf, made nontraditionally with brown basmati and wild rices, arrives punctuated with dried fruits and cinnamon.

2 tablespoons unsalted butter

1 cup (4 oz/125 g) chopped sweet onion such as Vidalia

2 teaspoons curry powder

1½ cups (10½ oz/330 g) brown basmati rice

½ cup (3 oz/90 g) wild rice

1 cinnamon stick

1 orange zest strip, 3 inches (7.5 cm) long and ½ inch (12 mm) wide, plus extra for garnish (optional)

4½ cups (36 fl oz/1.1 l) reduced-sodium chicken broth

½ cup (3 oz/90 g) dried apricots, cut into pieces

½ cup (2 oz/60 g) dried pitted cherries

½ cup (2 oz/60 g) sliced natural almonds

In a large, wide saucepan over low heat, melt the butter. Add the onion and sauté, stirring often, until golden, about 5 minutes. Add the curry powder and stir to blend. Stir in the brown basmati rice, wild rice, cinnamon stick, and orange zest. Cook, stirring, for 2 minutes.

Add the broth, apricots, and cherries and raise the heat to high. Bring to a boil, stirring once. Cover, reduce the heat to medium-low, and cook until the broth is absorbed and the rice is tender, about 55 minutes. Remove from the heat and let stand, covered, for 10 minutes.

Meanwhile, in a small, dry frying pan over medium-low heat, toast the almonds, stirring constantly, until golden, about 3 minutes. Remove from the heat.

Spoon the pilaf into a warmed serving bowl, discarding the cinnamon stick and orange zest. Sprinkle with the toasted almonds and additional orange zest, if using. Serve immediately.

Serves 6–8

Perfect Pilaf

This basic rice side dish can be embellished with vegetables, such as 1 cup (3 oz/90 g) sautéed sliced mushrooms, 1 cup (5 oz/155 g) sautéed diced bell peppers (capsicums), or 1 cup (6 oz/185 g) chopped, seeded tomatoes.

Preheat an oven to 350°F (180°C). Butter a shallow 2-qt (2-l) baking dish.

Rinse the rice, changing the water until it runs clear. Set aside.

In a frying pan over medium heat, melt the butter or heat the oil. Add the onion or shallot and sauté until softened, about 2 minutes. Stir in the rice and sauté until the grains become translucent at the edges, 1–2 minutes. Transfer to the prepared baking dish, add the hot broth or water, and stir to mix.

Cover and bake until all the liquid is absorbed, 25–30 minutes. Remove from the oven, uncover, and fluff with a fork. Season with salt and pepper. Garnish with the parsley and/or chives, if desired, and serve immediately.

Serves 4–6

1½ cups (10½ oz/330 g) long-grain white rice

2 tablespoons unsalted butter or canola oil

½ cup (2 oz/60 g) chopped yellow onion or 1 shallot, chopped

3 cups (24 fl oz/750 ml) chicken broth or water, heated

Salt and freshly ground black or white pepper

1 tablespoon chopped fresh flat-leaf (Italian) parsley and/or snipped chives (optional)

Mashed Sweet Potatoes with Brown Sugar and Nuts

You can use either yellow- or orange-fleshed sweet potatoes (the latter are commonly called yams) for this favorite family recipe. Walnuts, hazelnuts (filberts), or any of your favorite nuts, can be used in place of the pecans.

6 sweet potatoes, peeled

4 tablespoons (2 oz/60 g) unsalted butter, melted

2 1/2 tablespoons firmly packed brown sugar

1/2 teaspoon salt

2 tablespoons chopped pecans

In a large saucepan, combine the sweet potatoes with water to cover by 1 inch (2.5 cm). Bring to a boil over medium-high heat, reduce the heat slightly, and boil gently until the sweet potatoes are tender when tested with a knife tip, 20–25 minutes.

While the sweet potatoes are cooking, preheat the oven to 350°F (180°C). Brush a 1 1/2-qt (48–fl oz/1.5 l) baking dish with 1 tablespoon of the butter.

When the sweet potatoes are ready, drain them, place in a large bowl, and mash with a potato masher until smooth. Add 2 tablespoons of the butter, 1 tablespoon of the brown sugar, and the salt and mix well. Spoon the mixture into the prepared baking dish, spreading it evenly and smoothing the top. Drizzle the remaining 1 tablespoon butter evenly over the surface. Then sprinkle the remaining 1 1/2 tablespoons brown sugar and the pecans evenly over the top.

Bake until the sugar melts and the mixture is piping hot, about 15 minutes. Serve immediately.

Serves 6

Sweet and White Potato Gratin

In this contemporary version of scalloped potatoes, the orange-fleshed sweet potatoes and white-fleshed russet potatoes combine to make an interesting contrast, visually and texturally. This is the perfect dish for a large gathering.

Preheat an oven to 350°F (180°C). Lightly butter a 9-by-13-by-2-inch (23-by-33-by-5-cm) baking dish.

Using half of the potato and sweet potato slices, arrange them, slightly overlapping, in the prepared baking dish, alternating the white and sweet potatoes randomly.

In a bowl, combine the fontina cheese, goat cheese, Parmesan cheese, thyme, salt, and pepper. Stir to blend. Sprinkle half of the cheese mixture over the potatoes. Sprinkle evenly with the flour. Arrange the remaining potato and sweet potato slices on top, again slightly overlapping and alternating randomly. Sprinkle evenly with the remaining cheese mixture. Pour the cream and broth over the potatoes. Cover loosely with aluminum foil.

Bake until the potatoes are tender, about 1 hour.

Meanwhile, in a sauté pan over low heat, melt the butter. Add the bread crumbs and toss to coat. Remove from the heat.

Remove the potatoes from the oven and uncover. Sprinkle the buttered crumbs evenly over the surface. Return to the oven, uncovered, and bake until the top is crisp and lightly browned , about 25 minutes longer. Remove from the oven and let stand at least 20 minutes before serving, then serve directly from the dish.

Serves 8

1½ lb (750 g) russet potatoes, peeled and thinly sliced

1 lb (500 g) sweet potatoes, peeled and thinly sliced

1½ cups (6 oz/185 g) coarsely shredded fontina cheese

¼ lb (125 g) fresh goat cheese, crumbled

¼ cup (1 oz/30 g) grated Parmesan cheese

2 teaspoons fresh thyme

1 teaspoon salt

Ground pepper to taste

2 tablespoons all-purpose (plain) flour

1 cup (8 fl oz/250 ml) heavy (double) cream

1 cup (8 fl oz/250 ml) chicken broth

¼ cup (2 oz/60 g) unsalted butter

2 cups (4 oz/125 g) fresh bread crumbs made from 4 slices firm white bread with crusts removed

Garlic Mashed Potatoes

Roasting garlic in the oven mellows its flavor and brings out its natural sweetness. Adding it to mashed potatoes seasoned with fresh herbs elevates an old-fashioned favorite to a special-occasion side dish.

6 cloves garlic, unpeeled

2 tablespoons olive oil

1 tablespoon finely chopped fresh rosemary or thyme

3 baking potatoes, about 1½ lb (750 g) total weight, peeled or unpeeled, cut into 2-inch (5-cm) chunks

¼ cup (2 oz/60 g) unsalted butter

½ cup (4 fl oz/125 ml) milk

Salt and ground white or black pepper to taste

¼ cup (¾ oz/20 g) snipped fresh chives (optional)

Preheat an oven to 325°F (165°C).

Place the garlic cloves in a small baking dish. Drizzle with the olive oil and sprinkle with the rosemary or thyme. Cover with aluminum foil and bake until very soft, 35–40 minutes. Remove from the oven and, when cool enough to handle, squeeze the garlic from the sheaths into a small bowl. Mash with a fork. Strain the oil through a fine-mesh sieve held over the garlic and mix well.

Meanwhile, place the potatoes in a saucepan and add water to cover by 1 inch (2.5 cm). Bring to a boil and cook, uncovered, until tender, about 20 minutes.

Just before the potatoes are ready, in a small saucepan, combine the butter and milk over low heat, and heat until the butter is melted and the mixture is hot. Drain the potatoes, transfer to a warmed bowl, and mash well with a fork or potato masher. Alternatively, push them through a food mill or ricer placed over a warmed bowl.

Add the butter and milk mixture to the potatoes and stir until smooth. Mix in the garlic and season with salt and pepper. Stir in the chives, if using, and serve immediately.

Serves 4–6

Haroset

Haroset is one of the foods featured on the Passover Seder plate. A mixture of Red Delicious and Granny Smith apples is a good choice for this recipe.

3 apples, cored and finely diced

1/4 cup (1 oz/30 g) chopped walnuts or pecans

1 tablespoon granulated sugar

1/2 teaspoon ground cinnamon

2 tablespoons grape juice

In a bowl, combine the apples, nuts, sugar, cinnamon, and grape juice and stir until mixed. Transfer the mixture to a serving bowl, cover, and refrigerate until well chilled, about 2 hours. Serve chilled.

Makes about 2 1/2 cups (12 oz/375 g)

Cranberry Sauce

Cranberries are in season in November, which has made cranberry sauce a perfect accompaniment to Thanksgiving turkey. This recipe can be made a day in advance and kept refrigerated until just before serving.

In a saucepan, combine the cranberries, apple, sugar, and orange zest. Measure the orange juice and add water if needed to total 1 cup (8 fl oz/250 ml). Add the juice to the pan.

Place the pan over medium-high heat and cook, stirring constantly, until the mixture comes to a boil. Continue to boil and stir until all the cranberries burst and the sauce has thickened, 5–10 minutes. Remove from the heat and let cool.

Makes about 3 cups (1 1/2 lb/750 g)

4 cups (1 lb/500 g) fresh cranberries

1 apple, cored and finely chopped

1 cup granulated sugar

Grated zest and juice of 2 oranges

Desserts

Anise and Pine Nut Biscotti

Serve these firm, crisp cookies with a sweet after-dinner wine for dipping such as moscato, Sauternes, vin santo, or late-harvest Riesling. A dough scraper is the ideal tool for kneading this soft and sticky dough. A sturdy metal spatula will also work.

1 cup (5 oz/155 g) pine nuts

2 eggs

3/4 cup (6 oz/185 g) sugar, plus extra for sprinkling (optional)

1/2 cup (4 fl oz/125 ml) vegetable oil

1 tablespoon grated orange zest

2 teaspoons aniseeds, crushed

1¼ teaspoons baking powder

1 teaspoon vanilla extract (essence)

1/4 teaspoon salt

2 cups (10 oz/315 g) all-purpose (plain) flour

Preheat an oven to 350°F (180°C). Spread the pine nuts on a baking sheets and toast in the oven, stirring occasionally, until lightly browned and fragrant, about 8 minutes. Remove from the oven and let cool.

In a large bowl, combine the eggs, the 3/4 cup (6 oz/185 g) sugar, vegetable oil, orange zest, aniseeds, baking powder, vanilla, and salt. Whisk to blend. Add the flour and the pine nuts and stir until combined.

Turn out onto a heavily floured work surface. Using a dough scraper or metal spatula, knead until just firm enough to handle, about 10 turns.

Divide the dough in half. Form each half into a log 2 inches (5 cm) in diameter and about 13 inches (33 cm) long. Carefully transfer the logs onto an ungreased baking sheet, spacing them well apart. Sprinkle with additional sugar, if desired.

Bake until firm to the touch, about 30 minutes. The logs will spread during baking. Remove from the oven and let cool on the baking sheet for 10 minutes. Leave the oven set at 350°F (180°C).

Carefully transfer the logs to a cutting board. Using a serrated knife, cut crosswise into slices 1/2 inch (12 mm) thick. Arrange the slices, cut sides down, on ungreased baking sheets.

Return to the oven and bake until brown, about 20 minutes longer. Transfer the cookies to racks to cool. Store in an airtight container at room temperature for up to 2 weeks.

Makes about 4 dozen cookies

Coconut Meringue Nests

Here, meringue cookies are shaped into nests and dressed up with shredded coconut and jelly beans, making them an ideal addition to the Easter table or to any festive springtime menu.

3 egg whites, at room temperature

1/4 teaspoon cream of tartar

Pinch of salt

3/4 cup (6 oz/185 g) sugar

1 teaspoon vanilla extract (essence)

About 1/2 cup (2 oz/60 g) sweetened shredded dried coconut

1 package (13 ounces) large jelly beans, in assorted colors

Position 2 racks in the center of the oven and preheat to 225°F (110°C). Line 2 baking sheets with parchment paper.

In a large bowl, using an electric mixer on low speed, beat the egg whites until foamy. Add the cream of tartar and salt, increase the speed to high, and beat until soft peaks form. Add the sugar 1 tablespoon at a time and continue to beat until stiff peaks form, stopping as needed to scrape down the sides of the bowl. This step will take 15–20 minutes. Add the vanilla and beat until blended.

Using a large spoon, drop 6 equal-sized mounds of the mixture on each baking sheet, leaving ample space around each mound. With the back of the spoon, make a depression in the center of each mound, forming a nest shape. (Or flatten the mound with a table knife, and then raise the sides into a nest shape.) Sprinkle the nests evenly with the coconut, and then drop 3 jelly beans into the center of each nest.

Bake the nests for 2 hours. Turn off the oven and leave the nests in the turned-off oven for 30 minutes. Transfer the pans to racks and let the nests cool completely on the pans.

Carefully peel each nest from the paper, and arrange them on a serving tray. Add a few more jelly beans to each nest and serve.

Makes 12 nests

Spice Cookies

Although these carrot-flecked cookies are appreciated year-round, here they are decorated for Halloween. Use food coloring to tint the icing to any color you wish and decorate to suit any occasion.

Position 2 racks in the center of the oven and preheat to 350°F (180°C). Lightly grease 2 baking sheets.

To make the dough, in a bowl, stir together the flour, oats, baking powder, cinnamon, cloves, and salt. In a large bowl, using an electric mixer on medium-high speed, beat together the butter and sugar until well combined. Add the egg and vanilla and beat until light and creamy. Reduce the speed to low and gradually beat in the flour mixture until blended. Then beat in the carrot until evenly distributed.

Drop the dough by rounded tablespoonfuls onto the prepared baking sheets, spacing them well apart. Bake, switching the pans between the racks and rotating them halfway through baking, until the cookies start to brown, 10–12 minutes. Let the cookies sit on the pans for 1 minute, then transfer them to racks and let cool completely.

To make the icing, sift the 4 cups confectioners' sugar into a bowl. Add the melted butter, vanilla, and 1/4 cup cream. Using an electric mixer on medium speed, beat the mixture until smooth and creamy. If necessary, add more cream to make the icing spreadable, or more sugar to make it stiffer.

Using an icing spatula, spread each cookie with icing. Set the cookies aside until the icing is completely dry, about 30 minutes, before serving. The cookies will keep in an airtight container at room temperature for up to 3 days.

Makes about 20 cookies

FOR THE DOUGH

1/2 cup (2 1/2 oz/75 g) *each* all-purpose (plain) flour and old-fashioned rolled oats

1 1/2 teaspoons baking powder

1/2 teaspoon ground cinnamon

1/8 teaspoon ground cloves

Pinch of salt

1/4 cup (2 oz/60 g) unsalted butter, at room temperature

1/2 cup (3 1/2 oz/105 g) firmly packed dark brown sugar

1 egg

1 teaspoon vanilla extract

1 carrot, peeled and coarsely grated

FOR THE ICING

4 cups (1 lb/500 g) confectioners' (icing) sugar, or as needed

1/4 cup (2 oz/60 g) unsalted butter, melted and cooled

2 teaspoons vanilla extract (essence)

1/4 cup (2 fl oz/60 ml) milk, or as needed

Stewed Winter Compote

In this delicious compote, dried fruits are slowly poached in a citrus-flavored sugar syrup so that they retain their natural shape, texture, and color. For the best flavor, let the fruits steep in the syrup for several days before serving.

In a large, heavy nonaluminum saucepan over high heat, combine the water, sugar, and salt and bring to a boil, stirring to dissolve the sugar. Boil for 5 minutes, then reduce the heat to low and add the prunes, figs, raisins, apricots, cherries, and lemon and orange zests. Add enough hot water to cover the fruits by 2 inches (5 cm). Cover the pan and simmer until the fruits are nearly plump and tender, about 20 minutes, adding more water if the pan begins to dry out.

Meanwhile, halve and core the pears and the apple. Cut into thick slices. When the dried fruits are nearly tender, add the pears and the apple slices to the pan and continue to cook, covered, until tender, about 10 minutes longer. Transfer to a bowl. Taste and flavor the compote with brandy or port. Cover and let cool for about 30 minutes before serving. Serve warm or at room temperature.

Serves 6

3 cups (24 fl oz/750 ml) water

1 cup (8 oz/250 g) sugar

Pinch of salt

1¹/₃ cups (¹/₂ lb/250 g) pitted prunes

1¹/₃ cups (¹/₂ lb/250 g) dried golden figs

1¹/₃ cups (¹/₂ lb/250 g) raisins

1¹/₃ cups (¹/₂ lb/250 g) dried apricots

1 cup (¹/₄ lb/125 g) dried cherries

Grated zest of 1 lemon

Grated zest of 1 orange

2 large, firm Bosc pears

1 large Granny Smith or other tart green apple

About 1 cup (8 fl oz/250 ml) good-quality brandy or port

Cranberry-Raspberry Granita

Here, we combine a bit of summer in the form of frozen raspberries with the quintessential fall fruit, fresh cranberries. The natural sweetness of the raspberries marries well with the astringent taste of the cranberries in this deep red dessert ice.

2¹/2 cups (20 fl oz/625 ml) water

2 cups (8 oz/250 g) fresh or frozen cranberries

1 package (10 oz/315 g) frozen unsweetened raspberries, plus fresh or frozen raspberries for garnish (optional)

1¹/2 cups (12 oz/375 g) sugar

In a saucepan, combine the water, cranberries, the package of raspberries, and the sugar. Bring to a boil over medium heat, reduce the heat to low, and cook, stirring, until the cranberries pop, about 5 minutes. Remove from the heat and let cool slightly. Pour the mixture through a large sieve placed over a bowl, pressing on the fruit with the back of a spoon to force as much pulp through as possible. Measure 1 cup (8 fl oz/250 ml) of the purée, cover, and refrigerate until ready to serve.

Transfer the remaining purée to a shallow metal pan and place in a freezer. Freeze until the mixture is frozen around the edges but still slushy in the center, about 2 hours. Spoon into a food processor and purée until smooth. Pour back into the metal pan and refreeze until almost firm, about 1 hour. Purée again in the food processor. Then pack into a large plastic container with a tight-fitting lid and freeze until firm, at least 1 hour or for up to 3 days.

Remove the granita from the freezer about 20 minutes before serving to soften slightly. Scoop into stemmed glasses and top each serving with 2 tablespoons of the reserved purée. Garnish with a few fresh or frozen whole raspberries, if using. Serve immediately.

Makes 1 qt (1 l); serves 6–8

Quince Poached in Lemon-Vanilla Syrup

Quince is inedible when raw because of its intense astringency. Its flesh is white but turns a lovely amber and sweetens when cooked. The quince is a pome fruit like the apple and pear and, once cooked, resembles them somewhat in texture.

In a saucepan large enough to hold the quinces, combine the sugar, water, vanilla bean, and lemon juice. Bring to a boil over medium-high heat, stirring to dissolve the sugar. Then boil, stirring often, until a light-to-medium-thick syrup forms, about 10 minutes.

Add the quinces and reduce the heat to low. Add the grated lemon zest and poach the fruit, uncovered, until tender when pierced with a fork, about 20 minutes. Remove from the heat and let stand until the syrup is nearly at room temperature, about 15 minutes.

To serve, ladle several pieces of fruit into individual bowls or glasses with some of the syrup. Garnish with the strips of lemon zest.

Serves 4

2½ cups (1¼ lb/625 g) sugar

2 cups (16 fl oz/500 ml) water

1 vanilla bean

2 tablespoons lemon juice

3 quinces, peeled, halved, cored, and sliced lengthwise ½ inch (12 mm) thick

1½ teaspoons grated lemon zest, plus strips for garnish

Pears Poached in Red Wine

After chilling in the wine syrup, the pears are a regal deep burgundy. Don't worry if they are pale after poaching; they will absorb more color as they stand in the syrup. They make a fine dessert for a dinner party, as you can poach them a day ahead.

2 cups (16 fl oz/500 ml) light, fruity red wine

2 cups (16 fl oz/500 ml) water

1 cup (8 oz/250 g) sugar

8 lemon zest strips

6 firm pears, preferably Bartlett (Williams') or Bosc

Lemon juice to taste

In a saucepan just large enough to hold the pears in a single layer, combine the wine, water, sugar, and lemon zest. Place over medium heat and bring to a simmer, stirring to dissolve the sugar.

Meanwhile, peel the pears, leaving the stems attached. Add to the saucepan. Cut a round of parchment (baking) paper to fit just inside the saucepan and position over the pears. Adjust the heat to maintain a gentle simmer. Cook for 15 minutes, then lift the parchment and turn the pears in the poaching liquid so they cook evenly. Replace the parchment and continue cooking until the pears are just tender when pierced (they will continue to cook as they cool), 10–15 minutes longer. Using a slotted spoon, transfer the pears to a deep bowl or baking dish.

Raise the heat to high and cook the poaching liquid until reduced to 2 cups (16 fl oz/500 ml). Remove from the heat and let cool. Taste and add a little lemon juice if needed to freshen the syrup. Pour over the pears. Cover and refrigerate for 8 hours, turning the pears occasionally in the syrup to color them a deep red all over.

To serve, cut the pears in half lengthwise. Remove the core from each half with a melon baller or a sharp spoon. Put the halves, cut sides down, on a cutting board and thinly slice lengthwise, leaving the slices attached at the narrow end. Using a spatula, transfer each pear half to an individual plate, maintaining the shape of the pear half. Press lightly on the slices to fan them. Strain the poaching syrup to remove the zest strips. Spoon some of the poaching syrup around the pears and serve.

Serves 12

Caramelized Pear, Lemon, and Currant Tart

To make the pastry, in a food processor, combine the flour, sugar, and salt; process briefly to blend. Add the butter and pulse until the mixture forms pea-sized pieces. Transfer the mixture to a large bowl. Sprinkle with the ice water, 1 tablespoon at a time, tossing lightly with a fork until the dough comes together in a loose ball. Flatten into a disk and wrap in aluminum foil. Refrigerate for 1–2 hours.

Position a rack in the lower third of an oven. Preheat to 400°F (200°C).

To make the filling, place 2 tablespoons of the butter and 4 tablespoons (2 oz/60 g) of the sugar in a heavy ovenproof frying pan about 10 inches (25 cm) in diameter and 2 inches (5 cm) deep. Place over medium heat and cook, stirring occasionally, until amber in color, about 5 minutes.

In a bowl, toss together the pears, lemon juice, lemon zest, and nutmeg. Arrange the pears in a tight circle in the pan, filling in every space. Sprinkle with the currants. Place over medium-low heat and cook for 5 minutes, shaking the pan gently so the pears are coated with the caramelized sugar. Remove from the heat. Cut the remaining 1 tablespoon butter into bits, then dot the surface with it. Sprinkle with the remaining 1 tablespoon sugar.

On a lightly floured work surface, roll out the dough into a round about 11 inches (28 cm) in diameter. Fold in the edges 1/2 inch (12 mm) to make a thick rim. Pierce all over with a fork. Transfer the pastry to the pan, covering the pear mixture completely and tucking the edges inside the pan.

Bake until the pastry is golden and the juices are bubbling up the sides of pan, 35–40 minutes. Remove from the oven and let stand for 5 minutes. Invert a serving plate over the frying pan, then invert them together. Lift off the pan. Garnish with strips of lemon zest. Serve warm or at room temperature. Accompany with whipped cream, if desired.

Serves 6–8

FOR THE PASTRY

1 1/2 cups (7 1/2 oz/235 g) all-purpose (plain) flour

1 tablespoon sugar

1/2 teaspoon salt

1/2 cup (4 oz/125 g) plus 2 tablespoons cold unsalted butter, cut into small pieces

4–5 tablespoons (2–2 1/2 fl oz/60–75 ml) ice water

FOR THE FILLING

3 tablespoons unsalted butter

5 tablespoons (3 oz/90 g) sugar

5 firm but ripe Bosc pears, about 1 3/4 lb (875 g) total weight, peeled, quartered, and cored

1 tablespoon lemon juice

1 teaspoon grated or finely minced lemon zest, plus zest strips for garnish

Pinch of grated nutmeg

2 tablespoons dried currants

Whipped cream (optional)

Favorite Pumpkin Pie

Pumpkin pie and Thanksgiving are natural partners, but this pie would be welcome on any fall or winter holiday table. Serve each slice with a generous dollop of sweetened whipped cream flavored with a bit of vanilla extract (essence).

FOR THE PASTRY

1 1/2 cups (7 1/2 oz/235 g) all-purpose (plain) flour

1/2 teaspoon salt

1/2 cup (4 oz/125 g) cold unsalted butter, cut into 1/2-inch (12-mm) chunks

3–4 tablespoons ice water

FOR THE FILLING

2 eggs

1 can (15 oz/470 g) pumpkin purée

1 1/2 cups (12 fl oz/375 ml) half-and-half (half cream)

3/4 cup (6 oz/185 g) sugar

1 teaspoon ground cinnamon

3/4 teaspoon ground allspice

1/4 teaspoon salt

To make the pastry, in a bowl, stir together the flour and salt and scatter the butter pieces over the top. Using a pastry blender or two knives, cut in the butter until the mixture is the consistency of coarse crumbs. Sprinkle on the water 1 tablespoon at a time, stirring with a fork to moisten evenly. Add just enough water for the mixture to come together in a rough mass. Pat the dough into a flat disk, wrap well in plastic wrap, and refrigerate until chilled, at least 30 minutes or for up to 2 days.

Preheat the oven 425°F (220°C). On a lightly floured work surface, roll out the dough into a round 1/8–1/4 inch (3–6 mm) thick. Loosely roll the dough around the rolling pin, then unroll it over a 9-inch (23-cm) pie pan. Ease the dough into the bottom and sides of the pan with your fingertips, then trim the edges, leaving a 1-inch (2.5-cm) overhang. Fold the overhang under and decoratively flute the pastry around the rim.

To make the filling, in a bowl, beat the eggs with a fork until blended. Add the pumpkin, half-and-half, sugar, cinnamon, allspice, and salt and stir until all the ingredients are well blended. Pour the filling into the pie shell.

Bake the pie for 15 minutes. Turn down the oven temperature to 350°F (180°C) and continue baking until a knife inserted into the center comes out clean and the pastry is a rich golden brown, 40–50 minutes longer. Let cool completely on a rack.

Cut the pie into wedges before serving.

Serves 8

Fig and Anise Quick Bread

Offer a soft-ripened cheese such as Brie, Camembert, or St. André with this aromatic loaf for a memorable finish to a dinner. A dry red wine or a glass of port would be the perfect accompaniment.

Preheat an oven to 375°F (190°C). Butter a 9-inch (23-cm) round cake pan.

In a large bowl, combine the all-purpose flour, whole-wheat flour, brown sugar, baking powder, 1 teaspoon aniseeds, baking soda, and salt; whisk to blend. Using your fingertips, rub in the butter until the mixture resembles coarse meal. Mix in the figs.

In a small bowl, whisk together the 3/4 cup (6 fl oz/180 ml) buttermilk and the egg until blended. Make a well in the center of the flour mixture and pour the buttermilk mixture into the well. Stir the liquid ingredients into the dry ingredients just until blended and a soft dough forms.

Transfer the dough to a well-floured work surface and knead until smooth, about 20 turns. Form the dough into a ball. Place in the prepared pan and flatten to 1 1/2 inches (4 cm) thick. Cut a large cross about 1 inch (9 mm) deep into the dough. Brush with more buttermilk and sprinkle with more aniseeds.

Bake until the bread is light brown and sounds hollow when tapped on the bottom, about 40 minutes. Remove from the oven. Turn the bread out onto a rack, lift off the pan, and turn the bread right side up to cool. Cut into 24 thin slices and serve warm or at room temperature.

Makes 1 loaf; enough for 24 thin slices

1 cup (5 oz/155 g) all-purpose (plain) flour

1 cup (5 oz/155 g) whole-wheat (wholemeal) flour

3 tablespoons firmly packed brown sugar

1 1/2 teaspoons baking powder

1 teaspoon aniseeds, lightly crushed in a mortar, plus extra for sprinkling

1/2 teaspoon baking soda (bicarbonate of soda)

1/2 teaspoon salt

1/4 cup (2 oz/60 g) unsalted butter, at room temperature

1 cup (6 oz/185 g) coarsely chopped dried figs

3/4 cup (6 fl oz/180 ml) buttermilk, plus extra for brushing

1 egg

Pumpkin-Date Bread

The aromatic trio of cinnamon, cloves, and nutmeg enhances this rich-tasting quick bread. The recipe is generous: You'll end up with a loaf for brunch, one for the freezer, and one to give away.

1½ cups (6 oz/185 g) broken pecans

3 eggs

4 cups (2 lb/1 kg) sugar

1 can (29 oz/910 g) pumpkin purée

1 cup (8 fl oz/250 ml) vegetable oil

5 cups (25 oz/780 g) all-purpose (plain) flour

1 tablespoon baking soda (bicarbonate of soda)

2 teaspoons ground cinnamon

1 teaspoon salt

½ teaspoon ground cloves

½ teaspoon ground nutmeg

2 cups (12 oz/375 g) pitted dates, chopped

Preheat an oven to 350°F (180°C). Butter and flour three 8½-by-4½-by-2½-inch (21.5-by-11.5-by-6-cm) loaf pans and tap out the excess flour.

Spread the pecans on a baking sheet and toast until they begin to color and are aromatic, 5–7 minutes. Remove from the oven and transfer to a small bowl to cool.

In a large bowl, using an electric mixer, beat the eggs until frothy. Gradually add the sugar and then the pumpkin purée, mixing well. Stir in the oil.

In a bowl, sift together the flour, baking soda, cinnamon, salt, cloves, and nutmeg. Add the dates to the toasted pecans, then stir in ½ cup (2½ oz/75 g) of the flour mixture to coat. Stir the remaining flour mixture into the pumpkin mixture until thoroughly combined. Fold in the pecans and dates. Divide the batter evenly among the prepared loaf pans.

Bake until the tops are browned, the loaves pull away from the sides of the pans, and a toothpick inserted into the center comes out clean, about 1 hour and 10 minutes. Transfer to racks and let cool in the pans for 10–15 minutes. Then turn out of the pans onto the racks and let cool completely before serving.

Makes 3 loaves; each loaf serves 10

Sweet Cinnamon Almonds

These addictively fragrant almonds, served in small bowls with glasses of port, offer a memorable conclusion to a special repast. They also make a lovely hostess gift presented in an airtight jar decorated with a festive ribbon.

Preheat an oven to 350°F (180°C). Spread the almonds on a baking sheet and toast in the oven until lightly browned and fragrant, about 10 minutes. Remove from the oven and set aside.

Meanwhile, butter a large baking sheet. In a large, heavy saucepan over medium heat, combine the brown sugar, port, corn syrup, cinnamon, and salt. Stir until the sugar dissolves. Clip a candy thermometer onto the side of the pan. Cook without stirring until the thermometer registers 240°F (116°C), about 6 minutes.

Remove from the heat. Add the almonds and stir until the syrup begins to look cloudy, about 2 minutes. Spoon the mixture onto the prepared baking sheet. Working quickly and using a fork, spread out the nuts in a single layer. Let cool slightly. Break apart any nuts that stick together. Let cool completely. Store in an airtight container at room temperature for up to 2 weeks.

Makes about 3 cups (1 lb/500 g)

1½ cups (8 oz/250 g) almonds

¾ cup (6 oz/185 g) firmly packed golden brown sugar

¼ cup (2 fl oz/60 ml) tawny port

1 tablespoon light corn syrup

⅛ teaspoon ground cinnamon

⅛ teaspoon salt

Sugar Cookies

These classic cookies can be cut into nearly any shape and decorated as you like. For example, tint the icing with cold-weather colors for the winter holidays or pastels for spring, then decorate with the season in mind.

FOR THE DOUGH

1½ cups (7½ oz/245 g) all-purpose (plain) flour

1 teaspoon baking powder

¼ teaspoon salt

½ cup (4 oz/125 g) unsalted butter, at room temperature

¾ cup (6 oz/185 g) sugar

1 egg

1½ teaspoons vanilla extract (essence)

FOR THE ICING

4 cups (1 lb/500 g) confectioners' (icing) sugar, or as needed

4 tablespoons (2 oz/60 g) unsalted butter, melted and cooled

2 teaspoons vanilla extract (essence)

¼ cup (2 fl oz/60 ml) heavy (double) cream, or as needed

Food coloring, in a variety of colors

Colored sugars for decorating (optional)

To make the dough, in a bowl, stir together the flour, baking powder, and salt. In a large bowl, using an electric mixer on medium-high speed, beat together the butter and sugar until combined. Add the egg and vanilla and beat until light and creamy. Reduce the speed to low and gradually beat in the flour mixture until blended. Gather the dough together and divide in half. Shape each half into a disk, wrap separately in plastic wrap, and refrigerate for at least 1 hour.

Position 2 racks in the center of the oven and preheat to 350°F (180°C). Lightly grease 2 baking sheets. Place 1 of the dough disks on a lightly floured work surface. Using a floured rolling pin, roll out the dough into a large circle about ⅛ inch (3 mm) thick. As you roll, occasionally lift and rotate the dough a quarter turn to prevent sticking. Using a 2-inch (5-cm) cookie cutter, cut out shapes and transfer them to the prepared baking sheets. Set the scraps aside. Repeat with the second dough disk and transfer the shapes to the baking sheets. Gather all the dough scraps, then roll out, cut out shapes, and transfer to the baking sheets. Bake until golden at the edges, 10–12 minutes. Transfer the cookies to racks and let cool.

To make the icing, sift the 4 cups sugar into a bowl. Add the melted butter, vanilla, and ¼ cup cream. Using an electric mixer on medium speed, beat until smooth and creamy, adding more cream if needed to correct the consistency. To tint the icing, spoon it into 1 or more small bowls, add 1 or 2 drops food coloring to each bowl, and stir until blended. Spoon each tinted icing into a pastry bag fitted with the writing tip and decorate the cookies. Add colored sugars or other toppings before the icing sets. Let the cookies set for 30 minutes before serving.

Makes about 40 cookies

Warm Gingerbread

The fragrant personality of gingerbread—at once sweet, spicy, and piquant—makes a festive ending to special wintertime feasts. Serve alongside lightly whipped cream sweetened with a bit of confectioners' (icing) sugar.

Preheat an oven to 350°F (180°C). Butter and flour a 9-by-13-inch (23-by-33-cm) baking pan. Tap out the excess flour.

In a bowl, sift together the flour, baking powder, cinnamon, ground ginger, salt, cloves, and pepper.

In another bowl, dissolve the baking soda in the boiling water. Stir in the molasses and set aside to cool.

In a stand mixer fitted with the paddle attachment, combine the butter and brown sugar and beat on medium speed until light and fluffy. Slowly add the eggs, beating constantly. Beat in the fresh ginger and lemon zest. Using a rubber spatula, scrape down the sides of the bowl. Reduce the speed to low and gradually add the flour mixture alternately with the molasses mixture, stopping to scrape down the sides of the bowl often. The batter will be very thin. Pour into the prepared pan.

Bake until a toothpick inserted into the center of the gingerbread comes out clean, 30–40 minutes. If the gingerbread is browning too quickly, cover loosely with aluminum foil. Transfer to a rack and let cool until warm.

Cut the gingerbread into squares and place on individual plates. Serve warm or at room temperature.

Serves 8

3 cups (15 oz/470 g) all-purpose (plain) flour

2 teaspoons baking powder

1½ teaspoons ground cinnamon

1 teaspoon ground ginger

½ teaspoon salt

½ teaspoon *each* ground cloves and ground pepper

1½ teaspoons baking soda (bicarbonate of soda)

1½ cups (12 fl oz/375 ml) boiling water

1 cup (11 oz/345 g) dark molasses

½ cup (4 oz/125 g) unsalted butter, at room temperature

1 cup (7 oz/220 g) firmly packed brown sugar

2 eggs, lightly beaten

3 tablespoons peeled and grated fresh ginger

1 tablespoon grated lemon zest

Sugarplums

These sweet, spicy confections are the perfect conclusion to a special meal. The dried fruits and nuts can be varied. Apples, pears, and pecans are excellent alternatives. Wrapped festively in waxed or parchment (baking) paper, they also make a nice gift.

½ cup (3 oz/90 g) finely chopped pitted dates

½ cup (2 oz/60 g) finely chopped walnuts

¼ cup (1½ oz/45 g) finely chopped dried apricots

¼ cup (1½ oz/45 g) finely chopped dried figs

¼ cup (1 oz/30 g) finely chopped pistachio nuts

2 tablespoons brandy

1 tablespoon apricot preserves

¼ teaspoon ground cinnamon

⅛ teaspoon ground cloves

⅓ cup (3 oz/90 g) sugar

Line a small baking sheet with waxed paper. In a food processor, combine the dates, walnuts, apricots, figs, pistachios, brandy, apricot preserves, cinnamon, and cloves. Pulse until the mixture begins to clump together.

Using a teaspoon, scoop up a rounded spoonful of the mixture, press together, and roll between your palms into a compact ball. Roll the round in the sugar. Place on the prepared baking sheet. Repeat with the remaining fruit-and-nut mixture and sugar.

Refrigerate until firm, at least 1 hour. Store in an airtight container in the refrigerator for up to 2 weeks.

Makes about 18 confections

Oranges in Syrup

Navel oranges are in season from mid-November until late March, making this simple dessert perfect for both winter and spring menus. They are pictured here with chocolate coins whose circular golden shapes they mirror.

In a small saucepan, combine the water and sugar. Bring to a boil over medium heat, stirring constantly until the sugar has dissolved. Reduce the heat to low and simmer, without stirring, for 3 minutes. Remove from the heat and let cool completely.

Working with 1 orange at a time, cut a thin slice off both ends to expose the flesh. Stand the orange upright on a cutting board and cut downward, slicing off the peel, pith, and membrane in strips and following the contour of the fruit. Repeat with the remaining oranges. Cut the oranges crosswise into rounds.

Arrange the orange rounds in a serving bowl, and pour the cooled syrup over the top. Cover and refrigerate just until chilled, about 30 minutes. Serve chilled.

Serves 4

½ cup (4 fl oz/125 ml) water

¼ cup (4 oz/125 g) granulated sugar

4 large navel oranges

Beverages

Peach, Honey, and Cardamom Wine Cordial

This special cordial is really at its best during the warm weather months, when fresh peaches are in season. It is delightful as part of a Mothers' Day brunch or served outdoors as part of an Easter day luncheon.

Place the whole peaches in a large glass jar. Add the wine and cardamom pods; the wine should immerse the peaches fully. Cover the jar and let stand at room temperature overnight, then refrigerate for 4 days.

Strain the wine into a nonaluminum saucepan. Place over low heat, add the honey, and stir just until the honey dissolves, about 5 minutes. Remove from the heat and let cool. Stir in the vodka.

Ladle the liqueur into a clean glass bottle or jar. Cover and refrigerate until well chilled, about 2 hours. Serve chilled. It will keep for up to 1 month in the refrigerator.

Serves 6–8

5 large, ripe peaches, peeled

1 bottle (24 fl oz/750 ml) dry white wine

8 cardamom pods

1/2 cup (6 oz/185 g) honey

2/3 cup (5 fl oz/160 ml) vodka

Apricot-Champagne Cocktail

A glass of bubbly brings a note of celebration to any occasion. Add a splash of brandy and a bit of fresh fruit for special flair. Substitute peach brandy for the apricot brandy, if you like.

½ cup (4 fl oz/125 ml) apricot brandy, chilled

1 bottle (24 fl oz/750 ml) champagne or other sparkling white wine, chilled

8 fresh or frozen raspberries or 2 large strawberries, halved

Divide the brandy evenly among 4 champagne flutes. Slowly add the champagne, filling each glass. Garnish each serving with 2 raspberries or a strawberry half. Serve at once.

Serves 4

Holiday Cosmopolitan

A few frozen cranberries added to each glass make this festive cocktail especially merry. If triple sec is unavailable, you may substitute it with Cointreau instead.

1½ cups (12 fl oz/375 ml) cranberry juice cocktail, chilled

¾ cup (6 fl oz/180 ml) lemon vodka or regular vodka, chilled

3 tablespoons bottled sweetened lime juice (Rose's brand)

3 tablespoons triple sec

8–10 ice cubes

¼ cup (1 oz/30 g) frozen cranberries

In a large pitcher, combine the cranberry juice cocktail, vodka, lime juice, and triple sec or Cointreau. Add the ice cubes and stir to mix well. Strain into martini glasses. Garnish each serving with a few frozen cranberries.

Serves 6

Classic Eggnog

Cooked eggs and milk are folded into soft billows of whipped cream in this frothy version of the classic. A sprinkling of nutmeg and cinnamon brings a touch of spice to its creamy flavor.

In a small saucepan over medium heat, warm the milk just until it is very hot, about 5 minutes.

In a large saucepan, combine the eggs, sugar, and salt. Whisk until well blended. Gradually stir in 2 cups (16 fl oz/500 ml) of the hot milk. Place over low heat and cook, stirring constantly, until the mixture is thick enough to coat a metal spoon with a thin film or until it registers 160°F (71°C) on an instant-read thermometer, about 10 minutes. Remove from the heat and stir in the remaining 2 cups (16 fl oz/500 ml) hot milk and the vanilla. Cover, placing plastic wrap directly on the surface, and refrigerate until thoroughly chilled, at least 3 hours or as long as overnight.

Just before serving, pour the cream into a large bowl. Using an electric beater, beat until soft peaks form. Stir ½ cup (4 fl oz/ 125 ml) brandy, if using, into the chilled eggnog. Taste and add more as needed. Using a rubber spatula, gently fold the whipped cream into the eggnog just until no white streaks remain. Pour into a punch bowl, then sprinkle with the cinnamon and nutmeg.

Serves 12

4 cups (32 fl oz/1 l) milk

6 eggs

⅓ cup (3 oz/90 g) sugar

Pinch of salt

1 teaspoon vanilla extract (essence)

1 cup (8 fl oz/250 ml) chilled heavy (double) cream

½ cup (4 fl oz/125 ml) brandy, or to taste (optional)

Dash of ground cinnamon

Dash of ground nutmeg

Champagne with Raspberries

This classic combination makes a delightful introduction to any gathering. Pass tall flutes of the raspberry-muddled bubbly as soon as your guests arrive. You may use either fresh or defrosted frozen berries.

24 raspberries

6 teaspoons Cognac or other brandy

1½ teaspoons sugar

1 bottle (24 fl oz/750 ml) brut champagne or other sparkling wine, well chilled

In each of 6 champagne flutes, place 4 berries, 1 teaspoon brandy, and ¼ teaspoon sugar. Mash the berries gently with a spoon. Divide the sparkling wine among the glasses and serve immediately.

Serves 6

Ginger, Lemon, and Honey Herbal Tea

Choose a perfumed honey such as orange blossom for a beautifully aromatic result. For a particularly soothing variation, add a little brandy to each cup. Thin strips of lemon peel make a lovely garnish.

In a heavy saucepan over high heat, combine the water, ginger, and aniseeds. Bring to a boil, reduce the heat to low, cover, and simmer gently for 5 minutes. Remove from the heat and let steep, covered, for 15 minutes.

Add the lemon slices and return to medium-high heat. Bring to a simmer and stir in the honey just until dissolved, then strain into warmed cups. Mix 1 tablespoon brandy into each cup, if desired, and serve at once.

Serves 4

4 cups (32 fl oz/1 l) water

¼ cup (1 oz/30 g) coarsely chopped fresh ginger

¼ teaspoon aniseeds

3 lemon slices

3 tablespoons honey

4 tablespoons brandy (optional)

Indian Spice Tea

Serve this traditional Indian beverage as a soothing finish to any spicy dinner, or as a pick-me-up on a chilly night. Low-fat milk will result in a less rich but nonetheless comforting beverage. If you don't have loose tea on hand, substitute 6 tea bags.

6 cups (48 fl oz/1.5 l) water

5 slices fresh ginger

2 orange zest strips, each 3 inches (7.5 cm) long by 1 1/2 inches (4 cm) wide

6 whole cloves

Rounded 1/4 teaspoon fennel seeds

2 cups (16 fl oz/500 ml) milk

2 tablespoons tea leaves, preferably jasmine, Darjeeling, or Assam

1/4 cup (2 oz/60 g) firmly packed dark brown sugar

In a large, heavy saucepan over low heat, combine the water, ginger, orange zest, cloves, and fennel seeds. Cover, bring to a simmer, and simmer over low heat for 10 minutes to blend the flavors.

Add the milk and tea leaves and bring to a boil over high heat. Reduce the heat to medium-low and simmer for 2 minutes. Remove from the heat, cover, and let steep for 5 minutes.

Stir in the sugar until dissolved. Strain into warmed cups and serve at once.

Serves 6

Hot Double-Apple Cider

If the apple slices are very dry, you might need to add more cider after they have had a chance to rehydrate. For an especially warming variation, add a small shot of rum to each mug before serving.

6–8 cups (48–64 fl oz/1.5–2 l) apple cider

2 cups (16 fl oz/500 ml) water

1/2 cup (2 oz/60 g) packed moist dried apple slices

8 cinnamon sticks

1/8 teaspoon ground cloves

In a large saucepan over medium heat, combine the apple cider, water, apple slices, cinnamon sticks, and cloves. Bring to a simmer, cover, remove from the heat, and let stand for 15 minutes to rehydrate the apples.

Return the saucepan to medium heat. Reheat for 5 minutes. Ladle into mugs, distributing the apple slices and cinnamon sticks evenly.

Serves 8

Hot Spiced Rum Lemonade

4 orange zest strips, each 3 inches (7.5 cm) long and 1/2 inch (12 mm) wide

4 whole cloves

4 cups (32 fl oz/1 l) water

1/2 cup (4 oz/125 g) sugar

Juice of 4 large lemons, strained (about 1/2 cup/4 fl oz/125 ml)

1/2 cup (4 fl oz/125 ml) light rum

Twist each zest strip gently to form a soft curl, then pierce with a whole clove. Set aside.

In a saucepan, bring the water to a boil. Add the sugar and stir until dissolved. Remove from the heat. Stir in the lemon juice. Pour into mugs, dividing evenly. Add 2 tablespoons rum to each mug. Garnish each drink with a curl of orange zest and serve at once.

Serves 4

Caramel Coffee with Spiced Cream

A touch of store-bought caramel sauce swirled together with hot brewed coffee is delicious served with a dollop of cinnamon-scented whipped cream. Slip a cinnamon stick into each cup, if you like.

In a chilled bowl, using an electric mixer set on medium speed or a whisk, whip the cream until soft peaks form. While continuing to beat, sprinkle in the brown sugar and the $^1/_4$ teaspoon ground cinnamon and beat for a few seconds longer to incorporate fully.

Place 2 tablespoons of the caramel sauce in each of 6 coffee cups. Fill each cup three-fourths full with the hot coffee and stir well. Top each serving with a dollop of the flavored whipped cream and a sprinkling of ground cinnamon.

Serves 6

1 cup (8 fl oz/250 ml) heavy (double) cream

1$^1/_2$ teaspoons light brown sugar

$^1/_4$ teaspoon ground cinnamon, plus extra for garnish

$^3/_4$ cup (6 fl oz/180 ml) caramel sauce

6 cups (48 fl oz/1.5 l) hot, strong brewed coffee

White and Dark Hot Chocolate

To prepare the white chocolate, combine the white chocolate and the 2 tablespoons cream in a heatproof bowl placed over (not touching) simmering water in a saucepan. Whisk constantly until smooth, 1–2 minutes. Let cool. Whip the $^1/_2$ cup (4 fl oz/125 ml) cream to soft peaks. Add the cooled white chocolate mixture and continue to beat until stiff peaks form.

To prepare the dark chocolate, in a heavy saucepan over low heat, combine the semisweet chocolate and milk. Whisk constantly until smooth, 3–4 minutes. To serve, fill mugs with the dark hot chocolate, dividing evenly. Top each with the white chocolate, again dividing evenly. Sprinkle with cocoa and serve immediately.

Serves 4

FOR THE WHITE CHOCOLATE

1$^1/_2$ oz (45 g) white chocolate, coarsely chopped

2 tablespoons plus $^1/_2$ cup (4 fl oz/125 ml) heavy (double) cream

FOR THE DARK CHOCOLATE

7$^1/_2$ oz (315 g) semisweet (plain) chocolate, coarsely chopped

3 cups (24 fl oz/750 ml) milk

Unsweetened cocoa powder

Hot Spiced Cider with Calvados

Enjoy this soothing cool-weather drink in front of a roaring fire along with a selection of butter cookies and a bowl of fresh oranges. For a festive touch, garnish each mug with a cinnamon stick and a few whole cloves.

In a heavy saucepan over medium-high heat, combine the cider, cinnamon sticks, cloves, and crystallized ginger. Bring to a boil, reduce the heat to low, cover partially, and simmer gently for 30 minutes to blend the flavors.

Ladle the cider into warmed mugs or cups, adding some of the spices to each serving. Stir 2 tablespoons Calvados into each mug or cup and serve immediately.

Serves 6

6 cups (48 fl oz/1.5 l) apple cider or apple juice

3 cinnamon sticks

30 whole cloves

8 slices crystallized ginger, each about 1 inch (2.5 cm) in diameter

3/4 cup (6 fl oz/180 ml) Calvados or other apple brandy

Irish Coffee

Here is a variation on the drink made famous at San Francisco's Buena Vista Cafe, where it is a tradition on foggy evenings. It offers a classic cold-weather night cap to a cozy evening with friends and family.

½ cup (4 fl oz/125 ml) chilled heavy (double) cream

1 cup (8 fl oz/250 ml) plus 2 tablespoons Irish whiskey

9 tablespoons (4 oz/125 g) firmly packed golden brown sugar

6 cups (48 fl oz/1.5 l) hot, freshly brewed strong coffee

1 oz (30 g) semisweet (plain) chocolate, shaved

In a bowl, whisk the cream until slightly thickened. In each warmed cup, stir together 3 tablespoons of the whiskey and $1\frac{1}{2}$ tablespoons of the sugar. Divide the coffee among the cups and stir to dissolve the sugar. Top each serving with the lightly whipped cream. Sprinkle with the chocolate shavings and serve at once.

Serves 6

Mint Hot Chocolate

Whole milk makes a wonderfully rich drink, but low-fat milk produces a satisfying concoction as well. Add 1–2 tablespoons crème de menthe or crème de cacao to each mug for a grown-up variation. This elixir guarantees sweet dreams.

In a bowl, beat the cream and 1 tablespoon of the sugar until soft peaks form. Cover and refrigerate until needed.

In a heavy saucepan, combine the remaining 3 tablespoons sugar and the cocoa. Gradually whisk in the milk. Place over medium heat and bring to a simmer, whisking frequently. Add the 4 oz (125 g) chopped chocolate and whisk until melted and smooth. Stir in the peppermint extract.

Divide the hot chocolate among warmed mugs. Top each with a dollop of the whipped cream. Sprinkle with the shaved chocolate and serve immediately.

Serves 4

1/4 cup (2 fl oz/60 ml) chilled heavy (double) cream

4 tablespoons sugar

3 tablespoons unsweetened cocoa powder

4 cups (32 fl oz/1 l) milk

4 oz (125 g) semisweet (plain) chocolate, chopped, plus 1/2 oz (15 g) shaved

1/2 teaspoon peppermint extract (essence)

Basic Techniques

Peeling Tomatoes

1. Bring a pot of water to a boil. Fill a bowl with ice water. Immerse cored tomatoes in boiling water for 30 seconds, then transfer to the ice water.

2. When the tomatoes have cooled, peel off the loosened skins. If seeding is desired, halve the tomatoes horizontally and squeeze out the seed sacs.

Carving a Chicken or a Turkey

1. To carve a whole chicken or turkey, begin by removing the legs. Move a drumstick back to locate the hip joint. With a sharp knife, cut through the tendons and joint to remove the leg. Repeat with the other leg.

2. Next, separate the thigh from the drumstick, cutting between them down to the joint. Then, carefully cut through the joint and the tendons that surround it. Use the same method to cut off the bird's wings.

3. If you're carving a large chicken or turkey for serving on a platter, cut off the breast meat in long, thin slices parallel to the rib cage. For a small chicken, you can remove the entire breast from each side, starting at the breastbone and cutting down along the ribs to remove the breast.

Shucking Oysters

1. Scrub the shell with a stiff-bristled brush under cold running water. Using a folded kitchen towel, grip an oyster, flat side up. Push in an oyster knife to one side of the hinge and pry upward.

2. Keeping the blade edge against the inside of the top shell, run the knife all around to sever the muscle holding the halves together. Cut beneath the oyster to detach it from the bottom shell.

Working with Lobster

1. Detach the tail from the body and break off the end flaps. Using kitchen shears, cut along the length of the cartilage over the tail meat, open the shell, and extract the meat in one piece.

2. Pull the body out of the chest shell, then discard the white gills on the underside. Break the chest in half and use a fork to get the meat between the cartilage; you can eat the white matter, the green tomalley (liver), and any red roe present if the lobster is female.

3. Remove and discard the dark intestinal vein that runs under the body and the greenish stomach sac on one side of the head.

4. Break off the claws and joints; crack the joints and dig out the meat. Bend the smaller claw backward and dig out its meat. Crack the claws to extract the meat. Break off the legs, twist apart the joints, and pull out the meat.

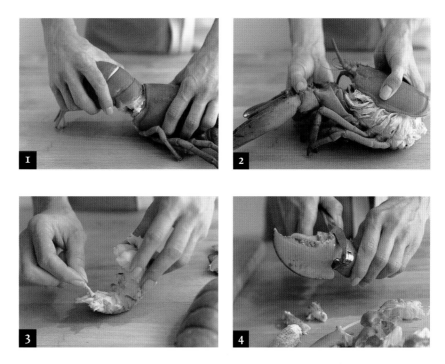

Glossary

Acorn Squash About 6 inches (15 cm) in diameter, this squash has a dark green, ribbed shell and orange flesh. It is named for its shape, which is similar to that of an acorn.

Arborio Rice This Italian variety has short, round grains that cook to a creamy consistency and chewy texture, making it ideal for the preparation known as risotto. Similar Italian varieties such as Vialone Nano and Carnaroli may be substituted.

Asian Sesame Oil The nutty fragrance of Asian sesame oil, made from roasted sesame seeds, enhances not only Asian food, but many Western dishes as well. Used primarily as a seasoning or condiment, Asian sesame oil burns easily and is rarely used for cooking. The Asian product should not be confused with the lighter, cold-pressed sesame oil sold in health-food stores and well-stocked food stores.

Bread Crumbs Fine dried bread crumbs are used to give a crisp coating to fried chicken and to add body to ground (minced) chicken.

MAKING FRESH BREAD CRUMBS
Trim away the crusts from $^{1}/_{2}$ pound (250 g) fresh coarse country white bread. Put the bread in a food processor and process to make soft fresh crumbs. Spread them out evenly on a baking sheet and bake in a preheated 325°F (165°C) oven until dry, about 15 minutes. Let the crumbs cool, then process again until fine; return to the oven to bake, stirring once or twice, until lightly colored, about 15 minutes.

Broccoli Rabe Also known as rapini, rape, or raab, this pleasantly bitter, strong-flavored green is actually a closer botanical relative to the turnip than to the broccoli it resembles. Its slender stalks, small florets, and deep green leaves have a strong, bitter, slightly nutlike flavor that goes well with a variety of pungent seasonings. You'll find it in farmers' markets from autumn into spring.

Butternut Squash Appreciated for its bright orange, sweet flesh, the butternut squash is cylindrical and up to 12 inches (30 cm) long, with its flower end slightly enlarged in a distinctive, bulb-like shape.

Capers The buds of a bush common to the Mediterranean, capers are picked when fully developed but still unopened, then preserved by salting or by pickling in a vinegar-and-salt brine. Used whole or, less often, chopped, they make a sharp-tasting savory flavoring or garnish.

Cardamom An exotic sweet spice, cardamom is a favorite seasoning in traditional baked goods of Scandinavia, Germany, and Russia. Its small, round, dark seeds are enclosed inside a dry, leathery, husklike pod that can be easily split open to remove them for grinding.

Celery Root Also known as celeriac or celery knob, this variety of celery is grown specifically for its root. The thick skin is peeled away to reveal crisp, ivory flesh with a sweet celery flavor. The flesh should be dipped in a mixture of water and lemon juice to prevent discoloration.

Fava Beans A specialty of springtime, these fresh shelling beans, also known as broad beans, resemble large lima beans and are especially prized for their sweet flavor when young and tender. Easily shelled by splitting the pod along its seam, the beans also usually require peeling of their outer skins, which, although edible, are sometimes tough.

Filo This Middle Eastern flour-and-water pastry consists of fragile, tissue-thin leaves that are usually layered and used as wrappers for sweet or savory fillings. Sold in the freezer section of well-stocked food stores, or fresh in many Middle Eastern markets, the dough must be handled carefully to avoid tearing. For easy handling, let filo dough stand at room temperature for 2 hours before unfolding. Cover the sheets with a lightly dampened sturdy paper towel or kitchen towel to prevent them from drying out. Brushing each layer of dough with melted butter ensures it will be crisp when baked.

Ginger Although it resembles a root, this sweet-hot Asian seasoning is actually the underground stem, or rhizome, of the tropical ginger plant. In its ground dried form, ginger is a popular addition to a myriad of sweets, although crystallized ginger—that is, candied with sugar—is also used. Look for the latter in specialty-food shops or the baking or Asian foods sections of well-stocked food stores.

Hoisin Sauce This thick, sweet, reddish-brown sauce is made from soybeans, sugar, garlic, Chinese five-spice powder or star anise, and a hint of chile. It can be thick and creamy or thin enough to pour. Used throughout China, hoisin sauce is rubbed on meat and poultry before roasting to give them a sweet flavor and red color. It sometimes appears as a condiment but should be added with caution, as its strong flavor can easily overpower most foods. Hoisin sauce is available in large cans, but smaller jars are more practical and are usually of better quality. Look for it in Asian markets or the ethnic-food aisle of major grocery stores. The sauce keeps indefinitely in the refrigerator.

Herbs

Using fresh herbs is one of the best things you can do to improve your cooking. Dried herbs do have their place, but fresh herbs usually bring brighter flavors to a dish.

Basil This spicy-sweet, tender-leaved herb goes especially well in dishes featuring tomatoes, as well as other vegetables, rice, seafood, and chicken. Beside common green basil, look for dark opal or purple basil, which has a spicy ginger taste.

Chives These slender, bright green stems of a plant related to the onion deliver an onionlike flavor without the bite. They are at their best when fresh and raw, as drying or cooking diminishes their character.

Flat-leaf Parsley Also known as Italian parsley, this variety of the widely popular fresh herb, native to southern Europe, has a more delicate flavor than the common curly type, making it preferable as a seasoning.

Marjoram This Mediterranean herb, which has a milder flavor than its close relative, oregano, is best used fresh. Pair it with tomatoes, eggplant, beans, poultry, and seafood.

Rosemary Used fresh or dried, the leaves of this Mediterranean herb resemble short pine needles set on a thin, woody stalk. It has a strong, fragrant flavor well suited to meats, poultry, seafood, and vegetables. It is particularly favored as a seasoning for chicken or lamb, and also complements pork or veal

Sage Soft, gray-green sage leaves are sweet and aromatic. Used fresh or dried, they pair well with poultry, vegetables, and fresh or cured pork.

Tarragon With its distinctively sweet flavor reminiscent of anise, tarragon is used to season many salads and egg and vegetable dishes, as well as mild-tasting main-course ingredients such as chicken and fish.

Thyme One of the most important culinary herbs of Europe, thyme delivers a floral, earthy flavor to all types of food, including vegetables, especially roots and tubers, and most kinds of poultry.

STORING FRESH HERBS
Wrap fresh herbs in damp paper towels, then place them in plastic bags and refrigerate for 3–5 days. Take care with fragile herbs such as chives and basil for they bruise easily. Trim stems from long-stemmed herbs to keep them fresh longer.

Once opened, transfer canned hoisin to a glass jar or an air-tight plastic container.

Horseradish Root A distant cousin of mustard, this root vegetable is powerfully pungent when grated, releasing intensely flavorful oils. Look for it year-round in farmers' markets.

Jerusalem Artichokes These tuberous vegetables, which resemble small potatoes, get their name in part because their flavor resembles an artichoke and in part because of their botanical kinship to the sunflower, *girasole* in Italian. They are at their best and most abundant in well-stocked food stores and farmers' markets during winter.

Juniper Berries This pea-sized berry from the evergreen juniper bush is blue-black and pungent. Juniper berries are used to flavor gin; in marinades for assertive-tasting meats such as lamb, venison, and boar; and as an important ingredients in sauerbraten and Alsatian sauerkraut. Use the berries whole; toast them lightly first and then crush them before adding to marinades or sauces.

Leeks Sweet, moderately flavored member of the onion family, long and cylindrical in shape with a pale white root end and dark green leaves. Select firm, unblemished leeks, small to medium in size.

TRIMMING & CLEANING LEEKS
Grown in sandy soil, the leafy-topped, multi-layered vegetables require thorough cleaning. Trim off the tough ends of the dark green leaves. Trim off the roots. If a recipe calls for leek whites only, trim off the dark green leaves where they meet the slender pale-green part of the stem. Starting about 1 inch (2.5 cm) from the root end, slit the leek lengthwise. Vigorously swish the leek in a basin or sink filled with cold water. Drain and rinse again; check to make sure that no dirt remains between the tightly packed pale portion of the leaves.

Molasses A source of rich, earthy sweetness in baked goods, molasses is a thick, syrupy by-product of refining cane sugar. Light molasses results from the first boiling of the syrup; dark molasses, which has a stronger flavor, comes from the second boiling.

Mussels Before cooking, the popular, bluish black-shelled bivalves require special cleaning to remove any dirt adhering to their shells and to remove their "beards," the fibrous threads by which the mussels connect to rocks or piers in the coastal waters where they live. For help with cleaning and debearding mussels, consult the technique section, page 275.

Nutmeg This popular baking spice is ground from the hard fruit pit of the nutmeg tree. For the best flavor, grate nutmeg as needed.

Oysters Buy fresh oysters from a reputable fish market. They vary in size from area to area. They are available live in the shell as well as shucked and in their liquor. For assistance in shucking oysters, consult the technique section, page 275.

Pancetta A specialty of the Emilia-Romagna region of northern Italy, this unsmoked bacon is cured with salt and pepper. It is sold either in slabs like bacon or rolled and is used to add a rich undertone of flavor to long-simmered dishes or stuffings. Look for pancetta in well-stocked food stores and Italian delicatessens.

Pearl Barley The nutty flavor and chewy texture of barley is a great addition to risottos, stews, and cooked then served cold in salads. Barley can be bought whole and hulled, flaked, and pearled. Most recipes call for it in the common pearled form, meaning hulled and polished to a pearllike shape and sheen.

Pearl Onions Pearl onions are small, dried onions no more than 1 inch (2.5 cm) in diameter. They are traditionally white, although red ones are now available. Boiling onions are also white and slightly larger. Both pearl and boiling onions have a mild flavor similar to that of green onions. They are often served as a garnish for stews, roasted meats, and marinated salads, or used for braised or creamed onions. Also available pickled or frozen.

PEELING PEARL ONIONS
Peeling a pile of pearl onions may seem daunting, but blanching them first will help the task pass more quickly and easily. First, bring a large pot of water to a full boil. Put the onions in the boiling water. Cook for 1 minute, counting from when the water returns to a boil. Then drain the onions in a colander. Rinse them with cold water, tossing continuously, until they are cool. Finally, with a sharp paring knife, trim the root and stem ends of each onion, then pinch to slip off its skin. Note that many cooks score, or shallowly cut, an X in each pearl onion's root end to shorten their cooking time, ensure even cooking, and keep the layers from telescoping.

Pomegranate Split open the thick, leathery skin of the deep red fruit to reveal an abundance of seeds—each surrounded by slightly translucent, ruby-red pulp—sectioned between tough white membranes. Its fruity, sweet-sour juice is used in stews,

Mushrooms

The popularity of all types of mushrooms has resulted in the successful farming of many different varieties, blurring the distinction between cultivated and wild. When preparing mushrooms, avoid washing them (with the exception of morels); instead, use a mushroom brush or kitchen towel to wipe off any dirt.

Chanterelle Wild mushrooms now also cultivated commercially, these pale yellow, trumpet-shaped specimens are distinguished by their subtle flavor.

Cremini Resembling common cultivated mushrooms in their shape and size, this variety has a rich flavor complemented by a medium brown skin and deep ivory flesh.

Morel Hollow-stemmed with oval honeycombed caps, morels look like trees in a fairy-tale forest. These much-loved wild mushrooms make their appearance in spring when they are gathered in the woodlands of New England, Michigan, and the Pacific Northwest. The meshlike flesh and empty core of the cap provides a hiding place for dirt and debris from the forest floor. Rinse well before

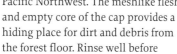

cooking, or even soak briefly if necessary, then trim the stems before using.

Porcini The Italian name for these wild brown-capped mushrooms means "little pigs"—an apt description for their plump forms. Prized for their tender texture and rich flavor, porcini are found fresh in summer and autumn. During the rest of the year, dried porcini are widely sold in Italian delicatessens and specialty-food stores. They are also known by the French as *cèpes*.

Portobello The flat, circular brown caps of these mushrooms, the fully matured form of cremini, grow as large as about 4 inches (10 cm) in diameter. They are enjoyed for their rich taste and texture when cooked.

Shiitake Parasol-like shiitake mushrooms were once found only in Asia but are now cultivated all over the world. The broad, flat caps have a firm, meaty texture. Discard the tough stems before using.

White Mushroom With their earthy flavor and satisfyingly chewy texture, mushrooms of all sorts can lend a robust, meaty quality to low-fat meals. You'll find familiar cultivated varieties at well-stocked food stores, greengrocers, and farmers' markets alongside many wild varieties—some of which are now commercially grown.

sauces, marinades, glazes, salads, and drinks. Pomegranate seeds add sparkle and crunch to salads and make a lovely garnish for soup. Use them, too, in tarts, fruit desserts, sorbet, or ice cream.

SEEDING POMEGRANATES
Working over a bowl, cut off the peel from the blossom end of the fruit, removing it with some of the white pith, but taking care not to pierce the seeds. Don't cut into the fruit with a knife. You'll break the seeds, releasing their juice and making a mess of your kitchen and clothing. Instead, lightly score the fruit into quarters, starting at the blossom end and working down to the stem end. Carefully break the fruit in half with your hands, pull back the skin, and remove the seeds.

Potatoes

Yellow Finn This variety of new potato is yellow in color. New potatoes are most often available in spring and early summer. They are low in starch and perfect for potato salad, roasting, grilling, and to use in creamed dishes, vegetable stews, and pasta dishes. A true new potato is freshly harvested, will have a thin skin, and will not keep long.

Yukon Gold Thin-skinned potatoes with a yellowish skin and golden, fine-grained, buttery-tasting flesh. These all-purpose potatoes hold their shape when boiled, and so may be used in all the same ways as red, white, and new potatoes, but they also make cheerful mashed potatoes and are good puréed with other root vegetables.

Prosciutto This cured ham is a renowned specialty of Parma, Italy, though it is produced in other regions as well. The hams are dry-salted for 1 month, then air-dried in cool curing sheds for 6 months or longer. The unique qualities of prosciutto are best appreciated when it's cut into tissue-thin slices. It may be eaten on its own or as a complement to summer fruits such as figs or melon, or it may be chopped or julienned and used in cooked dishes.

Prune Plums Prune plums are freestone fruits whose pits separate easily from the flesh. They also have a high sugar content that allows them to dry without fermenting.

Quince A relative of the rose, the quince has a heady aroma that can fill a room. These fruits, which look something like misshapen yellow apples, have hard, dry flesh and an overwhelmingly astringent flavor when raw. When cooked, however, the fruit turns a deep rose pink and increases in fragrance,

though it remains sour and need the addition of other ingredients to be palatable. Quinces are available from October through December; look for them in farmers' markets or specialty food stores.

Rutabaga This member of the cabbage family looks something like an overgrown turnip, to which it is closely related. Sometimes known as swedes, Swedish turnips, and yellow turnips, rutabagas come in a variety of colors, from brown to yellow to white. Their firm, yellow flesh has a strong mustardlike taste that mellows and sweetens when cooked. They can be substituted for turnips in most recipes, and cooking time will depend on their age and size, with smaller, young ones taking as little as 10 minutes and older, larger ones with tougher roots taking up to 1 hour.

Saffron Threads Perhaps the rarest of spices, saffron is derived from the dried stigmas of a species of crocus, sold either as threads or powdered. It gives intensely aromatic flavor and bright golden orange color to classic Mediterranean and Indian dishes.

Shallots These members of the onion family have paper-thin, copper-colored skins covering pale, purple-tinged flesh. They have a crisp texture and a more refined, milder flavor than the onion.

Shrimp Although often sold peeled and deveined, it's best to purchase shrimp (prawns) still in their shells if possible. Most shrimp have been previously frozen, and the shells help preserve their texture and flavor.

PEELING & DEVEINING SHRIMP Using your thumbs, split open the shrimp's thin shell along the concave side, between its two rows of legs. Grasp the shell and gently peel it away. Using a small knife, make a shallow slit along the peeled shrimp's back, just deep enough to expose the long, usually dark, veinlike intestinal tract. With the tip of the knife or your fingers, lift up and pull out the vein, discarding it.

Vidalia Onion Resembling large, slightly flattened yellow onions with their brownish skins and white flesh, these onions, grown in and around Vidalia, Georgia, are prized for their distinctively mild, sweet flavor. Other sweet onion varieties may be substituted, including Maui onions (from Hawaii), Walla Wallas (from Washington State), and some Texas-grown onions typified by the variety known as the 1015 Supersweet.

Vinegar Vinegar is made from a variety of red or white wines, and you will even find varietal wine vinegars in some specialty-foods stores. *Sherry vinegar*, a specialty of Spain, has a nutty taste and is especially good on vegetables and in dressings. In addition to wine vinegars, there are a number of vinegars based on grain and fruit, including cider vinegar and rice vinegar. *Cider vinegar*, a fruity vinegar made from apples and used in many traditional American recipes. *Distilled white vinegar*, made from grain alcohol, is used in pickling and in other recipes where its clean taste is desired. *Malt vinegar*, a mild vinegar made from malted barley, is popular in England. *Rice vinegar*, made from fermented rice, is widely used in Asian cuisines. *White rice vinegar* is milder than distilled white vinegar, and is used to add a slight acidity in cooked dishes and to make dressings for delicate greens. The Chinese make white, red, and black rice vinegars, with the deeply flavored black type used in cooking and as a condiment and the milder red type used in much the same way. Many vinegars are further seasoned by the addition of fresh herbs, fruit, or garlic, which steep for several days or weeks.

Watercress Refreshing, slightly peppery, dark green leaf vegetable commercially cultivated and also found wild in freshwater streams. Used primarily in salads and as a popular garnish.

Pears

The subtle sweetness and soft, juicy flesh of pears make them a luxurious conclusion to a meal. Three of the most common varieties used in this book are:

Anjou Available from autumn through early winter, these coarse-textured, juicy fruits have a rich flavor accented by a hint of spice. Large and plump, they have short necks and thin yellow-green skins. Also sold as d'Anjou.

Bartlett In season from early summer to early autumn, these medium-sized fruits are shaped roughly like bells, with creamy yellow skins occasionally blushed with red. Their flesh is fine-textured, juicy, mild, and sweetly fragrant. Also known as Williams' pears.

Bosc Long, slender, and tapered, Bosc pears have brownish yellow skins, slightly grainy, solid-textured flesh, and a flavor combining hints of butter and spice. They are harvested from late summer through early spring.

Index

First published in the USA by Time-Life Custom Publishing.

Originally published as Williams-Sonoma Lifestyles Series:
After Dinner (© 1998 Weldon Owen Inc.)
Chicken for Dinner (© 1998 Weldon Owen Inc.)
Classic Pasta at Home (© 1998 Weldon Owen Inc.)
Everyday Roasting (© 1998 Weldon Owen Inc.)
Fresh & Light (© 1998 Weldon Owen Inc.)
Holiday Celebrations (© 1998 Weldon Owen Inc.)
Soup for Supper (© 1998 Weldon Owen Inc.)
Vegetarian for All Seasons (© 1998 Weldon Owen Inc.)
Asian Flavors (© 1999 Weldon Owen Inc.)
Backyard Barbeque (© 1999 Weldon Owen Inc.)
Brunch Entertaining (© 1999 Weldon Owen Inc.)
Cooking From the Farmer's Market (© 1999 Weldon Owen Inc.)
Cooking for Yourself (© 1999 Weldon Owen Inc.)
Food & Wine Pairing (© 1999 Weldon Owen Inc.)
Holiday Cooking with Kids (© 1999 Weldon Owen Inc.)
Small Plates (© 1999 Weldon Owen Inc.)
Weekends with Friends (© 2000 Weldon Owen Inc.)

In collaboration with Williams-Sonoma Inc.
3250 Van Ness Avenue, San Francisco, CA 94109

Oxmoor House

OXMOOR HOUSE INC.
Oxmoor House books are distributed by Sunset Books
80 Willow Road, Menlo Park, CA 94025
Telephone: 650-321-3600 Fax 650-324-1532
Vice President/General Manager: Rich Smeby
National Accounts Manager/Special Sales: Brad Moses

Oxmoor House and Sunset Books are divisions of
Southern Progress Corporation

WILLIAMS-SONOMA
Founder and Vice-Chairman: Chuck Williams

WELDON OWEN INC.
Group Chief Executive Officer: John Owen
Chief Executive Officer and President: Terry Newell
Chief Operating Officer: Simon Fraser
Vice President Sales/Business Development: Amy Kaneko
Vice President International Sales: Stuart Laurence

Vice President and Creative Director: Gaye Allen
Vice President and Publisher: Hannah Rahill
Designer: Rachel Lopez Metzger
Managing Editor: Lisa Atwood
Senior Designer: Kara Church
Associate Editor: Juli Vendzules
Production Director: Chris Hemesath
Production Manager: Michelle Duggan
Color Manager: Teri Bell

Williams-Sonoma Special Occasions was conceived and
produced by Weldon Owen Inc.
814 Montgomery Street, San Francisco, CA 94133
Copyright © 2007 Weldon Owen Inc.
and Williams-Sonoma Inc.

All rights reserved, including the right of reproduction in
whole or in part in any form.

First printed in 2007.
10 9 8 7 6 5 4 3 2 1

ISBN-10: 0-8487-3195-6
ISBN-13: 978-08487-3195-3

Printed in China by SNP Leefung

CREDITS
Authors: Georgeanne Brennan: Pages 17, 21, 29, 65-66, 102, 123,149, 180, 187, 233; Heidi Haughty Cusick: Pages 87, 124-134, 195, 203, 213, 218; Lane Crowther: Pages 79, 100, 119, 161, 165, 199; Janet Fletcher: Page 234; Joyce Goldstein: Pages 35, 40, 80-84, 90, 99, 107, 112, 116, 162, 170, 175, 249; Pamela Sheldon Johns: 31, 46, 49, 62, 89, 93, 183, 192; Susan Manlin Katzman: Pages 34, 69, 76, 196, 206, 214, 220-221, 226-227, 238, 246, 253; Kristine Kidd: Pages 224, 241, 245, 250, 257, 260-264, 269-273; Betty Rosbottom: Pages 26, 44, 75, 152, 172, 229, 242, 267; Janeen Sarlin: Pages 108, 115, 120; Phillip Stephen Schultz: Pages 43, 138, 150; Marie Simmons: Pages 18, 22, 25, 32, 36, 50, 57-61, 72, 88, 94, 141-146, 155-158, 169, 171, 184, 188, 200, 204, 209-210, 217, 230, 237, 258-259, 266; Joanne Weir: Pages 39, 53, 191; Chuck Williams: Pages 103,104, 137, 154, 166, 176.

Photographers: Richard Eskite, Joyce Oudkerk Poole (recipe photography); Tucker+Hossler (cover)

Food Stylists: George Dolese, Andrea Lucich, Susan Massey, Pouké (recipe styling); Kevin Crafts (cover)

Weldon Owen would like to thank Ken DellaPenta, Melissa Eatough and Sharon Silva for all their expertise and hard work.

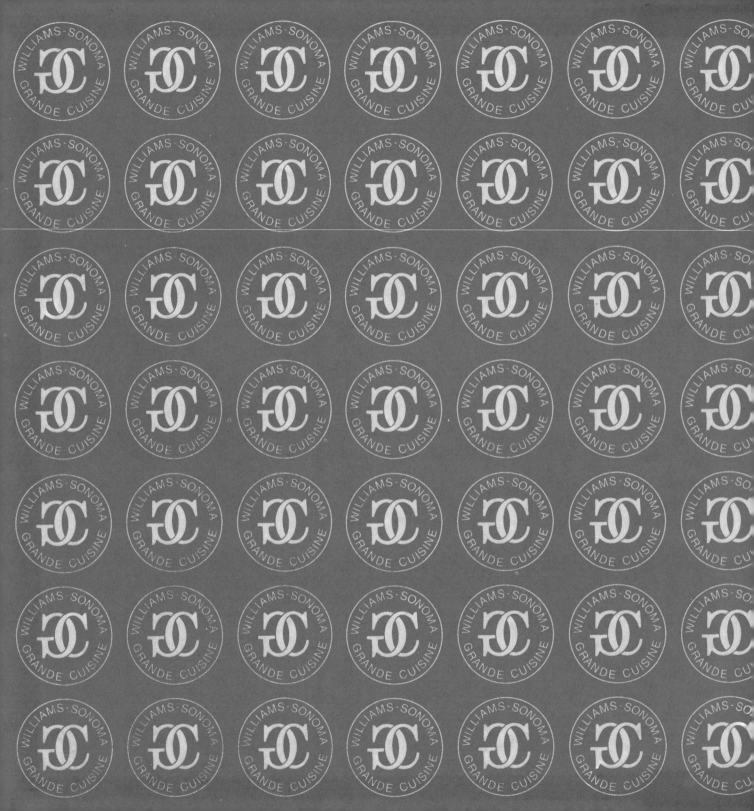